Sergio Siminovich • Rodrigo de Caso

BAROQUE POSSIBILITIES
How to prepare an 18th century oratorio

edipan

SIMINOVICH S. - DE CASO R.
BAROQUE POSSIBILITIES
How to prepare an 18th century oratorio
ISBN 978-88-905478-5-0

Original title: Un barroco posible: Claves para la interpretación musical
Spanish version: First edition - La Plata : Universidad Nacional de La Plata © 2013
Italian version: First edition - EDI-PAN srl, Roma © 2017
English version: First edition - EDI-PAN srl, Roma © 2017

Translation by Philip Salmon

Cover image by: Jimena Zeitune

We dedicate this undertaking to the titanic G.F. Haendel, in whose fire we were forged and to whom we owe the material for this book.
Special thanks go to the students of the last 22 years of the Chair of Choral Direction in the Faculty of Fine Arts at the National University of La Plata (Argentina), each course culminating in the preparation of a work of the baroque period for chorus and orchestra; and to the musicians of 50 seasons of oratorio (predominantly, and tendentiously.....Handelian!).
This little book is a summary of that journey.

EDI-PAN srl - Via Caposile, 6 - 00195 - Roma
e-mail edipan@edipan.com
URL: www.edipan.com

CONTENTS

As an attachment to the book is available the audio recording of the Oratorio Judas Maccabeus at www.edipan.com/ubp

Prologue

IN THE BEGINNING THERE WAS......THE WORD (St. John the Evangelist)

We have called our book *Baroque Possibilities*, because the true nature of the Baroque is great Flexibility of interpretation: this period allows the co-existence of different versions, both that of the musical score and of its performance. If we begin with the notation we can already see that it was 'approximate', a sort of *aide memoire* acting as a suggestion for extemporization. It is in a similar spirit of improvisation that we must approach these works, obviously within certain limits, without exceeding the confines of the harmonic and stylistic language of the period.

The objective of this book is to provide a practical guide to preparing an oratorio, the highest form of Baroque music, rich in possibilities (its major virtue) and in..... dilemmas!

The oratorio, indeed, is the most complete musical form of this period, but paradoxically it is performed less frequently than other forms because of an infinite number of obstacles, organizational and economical. It is our hope that this book will help to simplify certain aspects, and stimulate the enthusiasm that similar great works deserve. The book is aimed at:
- Choral directors who would like to lose the 'sociological' panic of conducting instrumentalists
- Orchestral directors who wish to discover the treasures hidden in the choral texts
- Vocal soloists who want to be more at ease with these epic works
- Instrumentalists who would like to learn more about period practice, or those who are already familiar with it and want to understand the grammar of its language.
- Choir members who wish to have a complete overall view of the greatest musical adventure of the Baroque: the oratorio.

The book is structured as follows:
- A. **Historical context:** we make some general observations on the function of the testimonies of the era (the Treatises) and on the crucial choices that we have to make today (eg. modern or period instruments), seeking to clarify by reasoned argument the different points of view that are held.
- B. **Dilemmas of interpretation:** we consider the different Variables (dynamics, articulation etc.), making a list of proposals for each line of argument, and showing that in reality they can also be applied in exactly the opposite way, yet still obtain a coherent interpretation: in effect the negative of a photo shows the image just as clearly as the photo itself.
- C. **Various items:** alongside these we consider subjects such as rapport with soloists, the positioning of the chorus, the preparation of the score etc. which are normally very important in the mounting of a Major Production of an oratorio.

D. **Analysis:** 221 extracts from one of the most exacting of Handel's oratorios *Judas Maccabeus*, shown as textbook examples of applied expressive techniques, which can be easily transferred to other similar works.

E. **Observations under the microscope:** in contrast to the previous rather randomly selective topic, we present a detailed dissection of a choral number and a solo number, attempting to balance meticulously the interpretation of EACH note.

F. **Appendices:** we outline some of the many subsequent topics that do not immediately appear the moment we enter the realm of baroque dilemmas. In particular we draw attention to the most fundamental: Ornamentation and Bowing.

A. HISTORICAL CONTEXT

Chapter 1: Treatises

Fortunately, there are many treatises from the baroque era that have survived. Fortunately?

First, let us consider the obviously positive point: thanks to these texts (given that composers did not normally add indications of interpretation) we have at our disposal a rich supply of information on many aspects of interpretation, allowing us, up to a certain point, to *deduce* the intention of works from so long ago. We say 'intention' and not 'correct interpretation' because the word 'interpretation' eloquently shows that its own application is relative. This opportunity to decipher (postulate?) the 'intention' can guide us and inspire us, and allows us to convey in the greatest number of ways our vision of a work, in the true character with which we want to direct it.

But we can also recognize a possible negative aspect: if we regard these tracts as a Bible, as it were, we could get stuck over contradictions that at first sight would appear to be insurmountable.

For example: Thomas Morley (1597) complained about musicians who "deformed" his pieces by filling them with embellishments and ornaments. What are we to deduce from such a position? That ornamentation was the general practice at that time, and that Morley, as composer, was complaining of excessive use of this habit? Or that Morley represents a general tendency of not ornamenting the original score?

This situation reaches its peak with Bach, who, with almost eccentric care, notated every embellishment, thus setting the boundaries of the interpreter's improvisation (this 'division of labour' is carried through to the 18th century orchestra, in which the instrumentalist is only required to be familiar with the technique of the instrument and not with counterpoint and composition; that is to say, without being asked to understand in depth the language that he or she uses!).

In terms of mathematical logic one could say that both options are valid: *A* and *not A*. In consequence, what we should not consider is an option *B*, which is the **total** exclusion of additional ornamentation, as we usually do as a matter of course from Mozart onwards, with a comfortable mixture of resignation and laziness.

There is another debatable aspect to the mechanical use of the treatises: if one or more of these writings indicates how to interpret a work with precision and an abundance of details...I, the interpreter, will face what could be called the 'Romantic paradigm', that is with a signing system of *crescendo, diminuendo, rallentando, caesurae*, etc., so complete that the result would be oppressive, almost anaesthetic.

This, in effect:

- would restrict my enjoyment as 'co-author' (see Appendix 3)
- would reduce my role as director to that of a mere translator of code... something like a teacher of *solfeggio*!
- would not allow me to take account of this baroque flexibility, significant enough for the great treatise writer Johann Joachim Quantz (1752) to

suggest that we vary the interpretation "during the course of the work" according to the expressions on the faces of the "audience in the second row…"

Also, best of all, we are able to deduce from these treatises that the shaping of Baroque phrases (articulation, microdynamics, accents) was much more detailed compared to later periods, perhaps because individual pieces from a baroque work are generally shorter in length and so require a closer scrutiny.
So, in truth, the best thing would be to interpret a work from the Romantic period with a Baroque toolkit, and not the other way round as mostly happens in some scholastic institutions and in the world of symphonic and operatic practice, even today.

Chapter 2: Instruments

We constantly find ourselves in a quandary: modern or historical instruments? (the description varies: 'original', 'ancient', 'period', 'philological' etc.)
Take a simple example: should we use a pianoforte or a harpsichord? The dilemma is easily resolved when put in these stark terms as, in order to realize the *basso continuo* of a Baroque piece, it seems more appropriate to use a harpsichord than a pianoforte, and already has seemed so for a long time. Indeed, many modern instrument orchestras incorporate a harpsichord into their performances of Baroque music.
But with regard to other instruments the boundary is much less clearly defined. Obviously the decision is down to individual taste: a director will feel more at ease with one of the two families of instruments, and this affinity will influence her or his choice.
Having said this, it is worth pointing out that, if cultural context and economics allow, 'period' instruments add a very distinctive timbre, filling the ancient notes with the magic of long ago, adding traditional spice to the mix and potency to the interpretation.
Besides, working with 'period' instrumentalists, who usually studied additional courses in their specific instruments, such as *basso continuo* or ornamentation, can often be a stimulating challenge: those being directed often know (or believe they know) the language better than the person claiming to direct them. So it is important to have at our disposal a good foundation in the baroque language (see Appendices), in order to be able to command a more legitimate 'authority'.
If instead we decide to work with modern instruments, it is possible to obtain a good approximation of *baroque declamation* with the following strategies, which are equivalent to an acceptable translation from one language to another:
- take account of the fact that the sound of period instruments is smaller. At the time they were played in churches (with the added benefit of their resonant acoustics) or in small halls suited to chamber music. Lesser volume implies a more refined execution of dynamics, just as the tuning of the violin is much finer than that of the cello.

- the 'baroquians' loved heterogeneity. In fact, in a period wind instrument the altered notes (that is those which correspond to the black notes on the piano) sound with less volume than the diatonic notes, because they are obtained using positions with less resonance (called the 'fork'). Rather than being a disadvantage, this irregularity, which we also meet as a certain swing in rhythmic patterns, constitutes an arsenal of subtlety and variation.

As to stringed instruments, how can we adapt modern instruments to the period sound? By limiting the use of habitual vibrato at specific moments and not using it, as in the eighteenth century, as a constant support for tuning as much as for expression. By eliminating *portamenti*: baroque musicians used open strings without restraint, leaving aside vibrato and embracing heterogeneity (since a note on an open string is much louder than on a stopped string). By adopting short bow strokes, with few slurs (omnipresent, on the other hand, in the Romantic era – see Appendix 6).

Other important strategies:

- don't stop the string at the end of a sound. The baroque bow finishes the notes like a tympanist ending his phrases without interrupting the vibration of the drum skin. In the same way use a 'detatched' style for the shorter notes, rather than the 18th century *legato*, and separate other note values.
- develop the expressive use of the right hand to enliven dissonances with a subtle *messa di voce*, instead of the left hand weighed down with the vibrato of prevailing 'modern' performance practice (see 2.4, number 11).

For wind instruments the means of expression is similar, with the added difficult and challenging appeal of adopting 'heterogenous' articulation for the quick passages (see Articulation).

Another important aspect consists in deciding with which forces to perform a work, whether dealing with a purely orchestral piece or dealing with an oratorio, which requires chorus and orchestra. Obviously small groups allow for a more detailed treatment. On the other hand, if we work with large groups we should try to lighten the density of sound, which can be achieved by reducing the size of the ensemble at certain moments. For example, in *Messiah* and others of his compositions, Handel indicates an alternation of solo instruments and the '*ripieno*'. As for the instruments of the *basso continuo*, if we do not have 'period' instruments at our disposal we could resort to a good quality electric keyboard, especially one with sampled sounds of historic instruments.

In short, as in many things in life, the form is important, but the content even more so!

There still remains the controversial question: why use period instruments (or imitate their particular sound) when we have at our disposal modern instruments that would guarantee a more advanced technique? Actually, there are experts who assert that modern instruments allow us better to confront the most difficult works in the baroque repertoire. But the inevitable question arises: would composers have written such virtuosic pieces, such as the violin concertos of Vivaldi or the Fifth Brandenburg concerto, amongst others, if they had not had adequate instruments at their disposal? Or if the performers at that time were mediocre, crude or sloppy. We don't have the answer...because we cannot fall back on recordings from the period. But we can guess that such a pyrotechnical and refined musical language might have in mind virtuoso interpreters, who also, as we know, constantly enriched the score with the appropriate melodic additions.

Today, fortunately, there are many groups with original instruments which have reached a standard of considerable virtuosity, excellent intonation and technical perfection and care of the expressive outline.

Chapter 3: Summary of Variables

For each of the topics that we will meet in the next chapters (Dynamics, Articulation etc.), let us consider a series of criteria that we could call 'bipolar'. That is, those which in practice could also be applied in the opposite way to that which we propose, yet still obtaining a coherent interpretation (as in the earlier example of a photo negative, which shows the subject of the photograph just as clearly). It is important, therefore, not to follow our recommendations slavishly as a 'recipe', but rather to have at hand a reference grid (like a fisherman's net) which allows one to identify and characterize the different forms of baroque language. Based on this grid, we can build our interpretative viewpoint, which, obviously, can be different for each conductor.

We can say that, within certain limits, the justification of a conductor is to have something new to say about a piece...that she/he has not composed!

So it is worth identifying and clarifying the various parts of the musical text (for example melismas, cadences etc.) in the same way that a theatre director transcribes the text for his actors using different colours – blue for adjectives, green for nouns etc. – according to their function, as in the use of initial capital letters for nouns in the German language.

So we speak of passing from *phonetics* – which in our analogy would be merely the pronunciation of the word – to *semantics*; the meaning of the music. And all thanks to our table of variables.

People could say, for instance, that we treat the listener as a baby trying to identify the semantics with utter clarity, as well as the grammar of the musical discourse. But we believe that, rather than being disrespectful, it might be advisable to treat the listener somewhat didactically, bearing in mind that on the whole a baroque oratorio uses an unfamiliar language from a distant time.

To return to the theatrical image, let us consider the case of two actors who, although they are not Norwegian, must present a play by Ibsen in the original language: we can clearly imagine the difference there would be between the one who had laboriously learnt the proper pronunciation, and the other who, as well as having an excellent accent, understood what he was saying!

Some of our suggestions are backed up by those mentioned in the treatises of the baroque period; in other cases we base our vision on considerations of what we shall call **CS** (basic *Common Sense*), reflecting the intuition that is evident in any coherent language.

B. DILEMMAS OF INTERPRETATION

Chapter 4: Dynamics

IN THE BEGINNING THERE WERE....THE DYNAMICS
From the very first note we are subjected to this Vital Principal: the sound is born, it develops and it dies. This is its natural dynamic span. A single note given enough dynamic is already Music: "the crescendo and diminuendo of a note is the basis of all passion", Caccini (1602).

From the very start we should distinguish between *macrodynamics* (levels of volume: *piano*, *forte*, etc.) and *microdynamics* (*crescendo*, *diminuendo* etc.).

1. It is important (and difficult) to establish an intelligent, varied and balanced macrodynamic for the more extended movements. Therefore, a long fugue should not trundle along always in the neutral world of *mezzo forte*. Also, it is fundamentally important to establish a 'macro-plan' for the whole piece, in order to allow an alternation of movements prevalently *forte* with others prevalently *piano*.
2. In a polyphonic composition we must decide whether every entry of the theme should be characterized with more emphasis in relation to the rest of the scheme. In 1592 Zacconi stated that the entrances of the theme should be emphasised in order to be better heard, and a century and a half later, in 1752, Quantz reinforced this idea, commenting that the secondary voice should sound more *piano* than the thematic voice. In spite of this, we could also apply here the photographic example we have mentioned, in that the theme also could be highlighted by playing it at a lesser volume in relation to the rest of the material.
3. And so we have arrived at the microdynamic, which is the essence, the key itself to baroque interpretation. It is obvious that microdynamics operate at a very subtle level. And while the image of the *photo-negative* works perfectly well in the wider field of macrodynamics, in the micro-universe some forms require quite a univocal treatment, as the majority of the rules that we will define are just as valid in a *forte* context as in a *piano* one.
4. In line with this book's objective, dedicated to the performance of oratorio (that is, compositions for chorus and orchestra), we have deduced our criteria mainly from the binary elements of *text*, those of phonetics and semantics. In fact, the fundamental element of baroque music is song. This also applies to the instruments, which, in spite of forging their own independence at that time, above all in the realm of virtuosity, are never disconnected from the rhetorical declamation of the word.
5. The mother tongue of baroque language, Latin, alternates strong and weak syllables. In general, the final syllable of a word is weak, and this implies that the ends of phrases usually need the effect of a diminuendo.
6. In the many places where the choral parts are doubled by the instruments, we very often find notes without their own syllable: logically, these notes should be played more quietly than those that have their own syllable.

7. And so we arrive at the heart, at the secret of baroque interpretation: the **melisma**. That is, many notes to one syllable. It deals with the higher plane of virtuosity, the exhibitionism that is so typical of the Baroque. Usually the melisma is found on the accented syllable of the most important word of the sentence. And so, what are our suggestions for the successful execution of a melisma? Emphasise the first note, that which carries the syllable, and perform the remaining notes with a lesser sound, but with a lot of subtle detail. For example, divide an 8-note melisma into five notes of *diminuendo* and three of *crescendo*. This approach would work well, for example, when the fifth note is the same as the first, and so does not carry any new information; or when, after a run of neighbouring notes, there is a leap between the fifth and sixth notes, hinting at the end of one mini-phrase and the start of another. Where there is a 6-note melisma, the usual division logically is 4 + 2. It is important not to accent the last note of a melisma, that which precedes a new syllable, so that the new syllable is clearly recognizable and facilitates the clarity of the word.

8. When part of an upbeat, repeated notes require a *crescendo* to increase tension. If they are solely part of harmonic accompaniment, a *diminuendo* is implied instead, with a small accent only when the harmony changes, and with a light *crescendo* to prepare the new chord. In sections where the orchestral accompaniment simply has a harmonic function it is helpful to distinguish the **dominant** with greater tension than the resolution to the **tonic**. Quantz (1752) states that the volume of each chord must depend on its degree of dissonance or consonance.

9. Do not accent the highest note of a figure (a tendency all too common in singers and instrumentalists alike), at least where it is not required by the text.

10. Long notes generally require a *diminuendo*, to allow the shorter notes in the other voices to be heard. Somewhat similar to a first read through where we might clarify the rhythmic discourse with a *pizzicato* for the strings or a light 'dum dum' articulation for the voices.

11. Meanwhile the opposite is represented by *messa di voce*: a long note that begins on a consonance and ends in a dissonance. We emphasise this with an eloquent *crescendo* which just stretches to the point where the dissonant note is about to resolve into a new consonance. This basic Baroque device would be lost if we used vibrato: the oscillation of the dissonant note would hide the harshness of the harmonic clash. We suggest using φ (the greek letter Phi) as a sign for *messa di voce*. Thus, with a specific sign the performer will know to play a particular kind of *crescendo*, motivated more by the harmony than the melody. In the 17th century Caccini (1602) and Fantini (1638) describe this effect, the former in relation to the voice, the latter to the trumpet. Later, in 1723, Tossi tells us to use this effect with moderation, supporting our point about the paradox of interpretative choices (see 1.1).

12. Given that we rely on the help of the sung text, as when the choral parts are doubled by the orchestra, it is not logical to emphasise those that belong to prepositions, definite articles or other parts of speech whose only function is to link words or phrases.

13. The subject of **Accentuation** is very important, delineating the art-science of accents[1]. We would suggest not distributing accents only as a means of demarcating the bars rather like bar-lines, but rather to group notes according to the inflections of the text, indicating the desired accents with longer and more incisive lines, avoiding, however, the use of always accenting in isocronic patterns.
14. Passages in triple time often suggest a treatment of accenting the even-numbered beats, while considering the odd numbers as an upbeat.
15. Every dance requires its own particular accentuation, and many choral numbers hide dances in their structural pattern.
16. To summarise, a basic dynamic hierarchy dictated by common sense (**CS**) would be:
loud syllable > weak syllable > melisma, where the lesser dynamic of the melisma is balanced by the greater richness of internal microdynamic inflexions.

Chapter 5: Articulation

IN THE BEGINNING THERE WAS....ARTICULATION
It was with this careful attention to articulation that the Philological Revolution began, distancing itself from 18th century Baroque interpretation.

This is a crucial subject, even to the point of the Centre of Ancient Music in Los Angeles having as its emblem a flag that says "Articulate!".
There are instruments, such as the harpsichord and the organ, that can 'suggest' a microdynamic only by using fine distinctions in articulation (or of 'density', which we will address in the chapter on the Basso Continuo).
Articulation is a fine art, like that of the goldsmith or the engraver. An analogy with sculpture might be illuminating: Michelangelo was once asked how he managed to sculpt such wonderful works, and he replied, "I simply release from the stone what is already there". Another illustration to help understand the sculpting and detailing of articulation could be taken from modern physics, which has shown that a solid object, a table for example, is in reality constituted of little material and much empty space, which defines its structure. In effect, articulation is the art of employing subtle and varied spaces of separation between the notes.
Let us look at some different types of articulation:
1. In general an accent will be more apparent if preceded by a gap (*caesura*), as if one were recharged with energy thanks to this micro-suspension.
2. It is usually better to separate leaps and to join the notes that move step by step, according to the inherent logic of each type of movement (Quantz).

---

1 "Accentics", coined by S. Siminovich, as a discipline proposed in his PhD dissertation. 2017, next to be published, giving ontological entity to the realm of accents.

3. We propose the following general rule which, allowing for some notable
    exceptions, covers a good part of the field: the smallest notes are often
    melismatic and, lacking their own individual syllables, should be kept as
    a unit, that is with a *legato* line for the chorus and a *portato* in the wind
    instruments:

while the strings are marked *alla corda* or *détaché* for the strings:

(examples taken from the oratorio '*Judas Maccabeus*', as are the majority
of our examples).

So, just as at the beginning of a movement there are the time signature
and tempo markings, we could also indicate in the score that the shortest
note value could be marked, for example, *portato*:

On the other hand, the note value that is immediately longer usually
has its own syllable and so corresponds to a staccato. In 1702 Brossard
advised: "in an *Andante* the quavers in the *Basso continuo* should be well
separated".

4. The fastest ornaments can be smooth:

unless you have the virtuosity to truly articulate each note (nothing beats
the almost hypnotic fascination of a rapid passage in which every note is
articulated). Where the execution is smooth it is a good idea to separate
the cascade from the arrival note.

5. One way to summarise the essence of articulation could be the italian:

Ba-roc-co

We separate the up-beat to achieve an accent on –**roc**-, and then join the next note to obtain the logical *diminuendo* on the weak syllable.

This example (apart from being an emblematic word!) clearly shows the interdependence of the two fundamental aspects of interpretation, **dynamics** and **articulation**.

And if we wait a microsecond before the second note we begin to see a link to the third aspect, **Agogics**, which we will deal with in Chapter 7.

6. We can also see here, for example, how it is more logical to articulate as if saying "Come Mariiiia" rather than "Come Mari-i-i-a":

Come, Ma - ri   -   a.

VERSUS:

Come, Ma - ri - i - i - i - a.

This helps to clarify our approach to the central pillar of the Baroque: the interpretation of the *melisma*.

7. Note that already by the 18th century wind instruments were articulating rapid passages by double- or triple-tongueing, creating a delicate and elegant *swing* of uneven rhythm (often referred to as the French term, *inégale*).

Chapter 6: Tempo

IN THE BEGINNING THERE WAS…TEMPO
More than any other variable, this term acquires a fundamental value. Music being
a temporal art, if we want to 'appropriate' a work that we have not composed
we must above all 'own' the tempo, choosing the best Possible Tempo.

The choice of a good tempo is generally very complex and has to take into
consideration various details. Bemetzreider (1771) took it to eloquent extremes
when he said "taste is the true metronome".
How do we find the criteria in order not to leave the choice of a good tempo
merely to personal taste? We would suggest selecting a key figure or phrase from
which to decide the tempo, that is, not just following that apparently suggested by
the first few bars, a comfortable route, but not always effective. Leopold Mozart
(1756) stated that "every melodic piece contains at least one phrase that allows
us to recognize the ideal tempo".
Here are some methods which can guide us in the right direction:

1. Bear in mind the tempo marking of the composer - although in the Baroque
    these indications can be very variable, elastic or…non-existent!

2. Avoid the extremes of excessively slow or excessively fast movements. We
    can state that in the baroque period the spectrum of possible speeds was
    small in the absolute sense, and this could imply that the micro-oscillations
    would be greater in the relative sense, as we have seen when talking
    of dynamics. Ignore the temptation to take tempi that are excessively
    broad (a 'modern' pretext to show breath capacity or bow control) or
    vertiginously fast (an excuse to exhibit digital virtuosity). In other words,
    follow the path shown by Couperin "I like more that which moves me
    than that which surprises me".

3. The flexibility of tempi is mentioned in an infinite number of documents.
    Frescobaldi (1615) decreed that "in my Toccatas and Madrigals it is
    permitted to modify the tempo in different sections". The concept of
    flexibility embraces all of this repertoire, and apart from anything else is
    one of the great reasons to come back to it again and again. This concept
    will be developed further in the next chapter (7. *Agogics*). In a wider
    application, this flexibility is also evident in the flexibility facilitated by the
    specific choice of tempo, which can also be based on:
    a. The acoustical characteristics of the concert venue.
    b. The number of musicians.
    c. The technical ability of the performers.
    d. In longer works (oratorios, Passions etc.) judge the speed of a
        movement according to those either side, to create balance and
        contrast. This requires a careful and detailed distribution of relative
        speeds.

4.   We can also refer to the famous treatise of Quantz for choice of tempo, where, like a metronome before its time (it was patented in 1812), the speeds of the various dances are suggested by taking the unit of measure as the normal rate of the heartbeat (70 per minute).

5.   We see that several paradoxes can arise when considering Tempo.
    a.   The scansion (the 'beating' of a bar) could be much less than in Romanticism (in more correct terminology: with fewer subdivisions). For example, in the Sinfonia of Handel's *Messiah*:

a 'Romantic' conductor would beat in 8, while one more familiar with baroque music would beat in 4; while in the baroque period he would probably beat....in 2!

    b.   The pulse is smaller than in Romanticism. For example, an *Allegro* in 4, which would probably be beaten as 4 crotchets to a bar, often 'pulses' instead in quavers according to the basso continuo.
    c.   The adoption of a new speed should surprise but not upset the listener. On the other hand, a tempo that is constant and regular (like, for example, that of a *Passacaglia*, a *Chaconne* or a *basso ostinato*) should not lull to sleep, but hypnotise.

6.   **CS**: as performer I must be able to adapt my interpretation (incorporating its variables of dynamics, articulation, ornamentation etc.) to WHATEVER speed. It is good practise, particularly useful for soloists, given that conductors often take tempi that the soloist might find uncomfortable or unfamiliar, or with which he or she may not agree (which obviously could lead to the usual tensions). The wise Quantz (1752) came to the conclusion that if the conductor sets an incorrect speed, it is the right and responsibility of the soloist to correct it by changing the speed directly when the solo passage begins. A singer or an instrumental soloist at the mercy of a particularly uncomfortable speed should have ready various survival techniques: to decide which notes to miss out if defeated by the speed, what extra breaths to take etc.

Chapter 7: Agogics

IN THE BEGINNING THERE WERE….AGOGICS
If I am slave to the Tempo, I am an Object. Only by controlling the instants, the moments, do I become the Subject. The subject of Agogics is the meeting point between Heraclitus and Parmenides.

Agogics (a term first used by Hugo Riemann in 1893), which are those small variations in tempo not written in the score but which are indispensable for the execution of a work, are to Tempo as Micro-dynamics are to Macro-dynamics. It is the realm of subtle and microscopic fluctuations of speed. For the purposes of the Baroque we can say that:

1. A *ritenuto* is more appropriate than a *rallentando*, and is very effective to establish punctuation marks:
    a. At cadenzas, to separate and shape phrases and sections
    b. In polyphonic sections, to direct the listeners' attention before the entrance of a voice
    c. Before an accent, to underline the orgasmic process of tension-release
    d. Before the final note.
2. Obviously homophony allows for more agogic freedom than polyphony, although the best baroque ensembles manage to produce a very elastic *swing* (confirming the old adage: the most important attribute for a musician is to know how to listen). Agogics also oblige the spectator to listen more closely.
3. Baroque notation being merely a rough outline, a figure such as this:

    does not necessarily require exact proportions, and is more eloquently expressed simply as a long note followed by five shorter notes, or as two gestures contained in a *tactus* of a minim. Defining a single gesture thus becomes more than a sum of its parts of individual notes (a rather unpleasant image will enable us to remember indelibly this sort of *swing*: how in capitalist society the rich become richer and the poor become….poorer). This is the rhythmic stylization that gives *swing* to this type of rhythmic figure.
4. Agogics are the territory of good taste, of exquisite subtlety in relation to the beat. C.P.E. Bach (1753) said in this regard: "certain variations of the pulse are extremely pleasing, but it is advisable to avoid excessive and exaggerated *ritenuti*". We suggest the following symbol for these microscopic moments of sustaining:

    ['coroncina']

5. The linking bridges are generally slightly *rubato*.
6. **CS**: we know that baroque repertoire is subject to the fires of improvisation (in fact....it is greedy for them!). Therefore in performance I must convey the idea of extemporizing ('recite' instead of 'read'). To understand this point better, think of an extreme analogy: imagine the effect of a declaration of love, pedantically....READ!

Chapter 8: Text

IN THE BEGINNING THERE WAS....THE TEXT.
Music gives words a context. This marriage reaches its height in the Baroque and flourishes with the growing emancipation of the instruments.

We touch on a very important element here, because we are dealing with oratorio, that is, music for **choir** and orchestra.
1. Above all, pay close attention to **pronunciation**: enunciate the consonants well, without falling into scholastic declamation. This relates to the detailed observations that we introduced in the first section of the chapter on Articulation. And in the same way that the singer (solo or choral) should enunciate the text clearly, the instrumentalist should pay detailed attention to articulation. Unlike the singer, the instrumentalist does not have the text to help him, but can enhance his understanding with the innumerable examples found in the oratorio repertoire: voices and instruments often move together, doubling or imitating each other. Singing teachers proudly emphasise the importance of the vowels (warm, rich, free), but the aforementioned 'Michaelangelo effect' is achieved above all by a good articulation of the consonants. An important function of the conductor is to infuse those being directed with the sensual pleasure of the text. Bear in mind that badly enunciated text will sound amorphous. For example:
      "o-o-a a i-o-a oo u-e-a e oo-i"
   instead of the clear phrase *"Consonants are important to understand the music"*.
2. Let us now consider the **semantics** (in one of the appendices we mention a more specific aspect: that most baroque "Theory of Affect". Let us take as an example the simple phrase:
      I am telling you that I have bought a house.
   Semantically, I can alter the emphasis of the phrase by choosing which element to emphasise:
      *I am **telling** you that I have bought a house.*
      *I am telling **you** that I have bought a house.*
      *I am telling you that I **have** bought a house.*
      *I am telling you that I have bought a **house**.*
   And every option changes the meaning. It also becomes evident that there is no sense at all in emphasizing the preposition "that", as already mentioned in Chapter 2.1 at point 12 on articles, prepositions and conjunctives.

3.   Now let us consider a very common occurence, which almost acts as a crutch for conductors: putting the final consonant on the following rest. In this example, the word "Gott":

This system is very practical, representing a generally agreed convention, and thus avoiding a proliferation of gestures specifically for pronunciation.... but it is unnatural! Nobody speaks like that. And this shows once more that writing in the Baroque period is only an approximate guide.

Chapter 9: Ornamentation

IN THE BEGINNING THERE WAS....ORNAMENTATION
Music that LIVES should sound as though it were born the moment it is heard. A convincing orator prepares his delivery with a few word-headings, which he enriches according to his perception of the listening public.

Two schools have made their mark on the Baroque: the French school, which expects understated detailed embellishments appropriate to the context; and the Italian school, which uses variations on the melody with great freedom, based on the general harmonic architecture.

1.   The most common obligatory embellishment is the **trill**. Its function is structural, closing phrases and half-phrases like a form of punctuation. But it is rather like a flirtation, pleased with itself, daring to oscillate boldly between two notes. We could say that it is a single note formed in reality of two notes! It needs to be practiced so that its execution does not sound mechanical. It is often not indicated, but everyone knows that they must use a trill to conclude a phrase or a section. It begins on the upper note (the **appoggiatura**, which, as we will see in the next point, is not usually even indicated in the score), creating a dissonance with the harmony in the other parts; it then oscillates between the two notes and finally resolves on the last note, and if we are in a slow movement, anticipating it.

The oscillation should reflect the *flexibility* that we have already mentioned, because the speed is not constant: it gets faster until the oscillation implodes, and the dynamics accompany this process with a similar fluctuation.

There are three types of trill: the most common, and best known, is the *harmonic trill* (at cadences and half-cadences); less often we see the *melodic trill*, generally accompanied by an elegant adjoining bridge. We can see an example of this in the *Grande Entreé* in Handel's *Alceste*:

Finally, there is the trill that functions purely dynamically, like a pyrotechnical accent, used especially in triumphal marches and in more solemn numbers. It is interesting (paradox or subtle irony?) that such martial music should display these flashes of extreme luminosity.

2. An embellishment closely related to the trill, almost its genetic embryo, is the **appoggiatura**. It can be the note above or below that written in the score, adjoining itself as a support, dissonance or harmonic "smudge" preceding the written note and delaying its arrival. While the trill announces the end of a phrase, the appoggiatura on its own is used to give emphasis, capturing the attention and bringing the phrase into sharp relief.
3. Italian ornamentation is bold, creative, fantastical. It is better not to exaggerate too profusely, as too much exhibitionism could obscure the musical discourse. But a certain dose of passion is necessary: this way the

listener feels 'ravished' by the performer. In this area, rather than mere good taste (the stilted parent of Common Sense), we should submerge ourselves in *identification* with the composer (see Appendix 4).

4. Perhaps a linguistic example can clarify the difference.
    Starting with a simple phrase:
    "I took your hand".
    in French ornamentation it might be embellished thus:
    "Your hand I took in mine"
    while in the Italian style it might be:
    "My fingers intertwined with yours".

5. The best way to have ornamentation appropriate to the baroque period 'in the ear' or under the fingers, and not that more suited to other periods, is to study compositions that are already ornamented (for example the ornaments that J. S. Bach wrote to Benedetto Marcello's *Adagio*) and to write exercises in that style. We can also find help in the form of *Variations*: there are infinite examples, like Handel's *Cello Suites*, *Variazioni sul tema della Follia* by Corelli, Vivaldi, Geminiani etc.

6. *CS*: ornamentation should add beauty, not take it away. Nor should it ever be a means of covering a deficiency in expression by being unable to give a phrase an interesting expressive shape. *Obbligatory embellishments* are like Galateo's *Rules of Polite Behaviour*: always to be present and, so as not to lack content, embellishing the *form* with care and finesse. On the other hand, with *improvised embellishments* the listener should not be able to distinguish between the composer and the interpreter (above all in the *Da capo*, which should be ornamented but without departing from the *feeling* implicit in the musical writing).

Chapter 10: Basso continuo

IN THE BEGINNING THERE WAS....BASSO CONTINUO
Without this structural element the entire construction of a baroque composition wobbles. From this harmonic foundation we build our expressive plan.

The Baroque era is also known as 'the age of the continuo'. The use of harmony instruments as the support of the melodic discourse is the quintessence of this repertoire.

The continuo bass can also be played by melodic instruments ('cello, viola da gamba, bassoon) but it is the instruments of harmony (harpsichord, organ, theorbo, lute, baroque guitar etc.) that realize the task more assiduously. In fact, as the chords can be indicated in codified form - called 'figured bass' - we usually find only the bass line in the score (in the left hand for keyboard instruments) and it is the continuo players, with their complete knowledge of the language of baroque music, who must deduce or 'invent' the chords according to their various functions: accompany the soloists, form bridges between phrases, support the choir, create atmosphere in the recitatives etc.

Very often the continuo player is the true protagonist of the oratorio. Indeed the director and continuo player are often the same person.

1. Let us look at some basic rules:
    a. Locke (1672): *"in order to avoid consecutive fifths and octaves, the player is advised to adopt contrary motion between the two hands"*
    b. Saint-Lambert (1707): *"....move the hands from one chord to the next with the greatest economy of fingering"*
    c. Quantz (1752): *"The norm is to play in four parts, and even when it is necessary to break this rule, one should reduce or increase the number of parts only to obtain a good musical effect"* (in modern terms we would say, emphasise the dynamics by modifying the density).
2. Resources for the continuo player:
    The arpeggio, to accent, emphasise, underline:

Bridges, to join two sections:

Ejecución

Continuo

The correct adjustment of density of sound (with the resultant effect on dynamics):

Esecuzione

Continuo

Rhythmic impulse: as in a fanfare (or like a jazz drummer):

Played

Writen

3. The director should mark as much as possible in the continuo player's score (likewise, the continuo player, using his own judgement, should characterize the work according to his OWN ideas and imagination!). This exhaustive planning of the score, which the director should prepare in advance, includes what we shall call the *Harmonic Rhythm* (to establish which notes of the bass line should be harmonized). Such preparatory work becomes indispensable when there is more than one continuo player and we want grammatical agreement, that is a homogeneity of figuring. Unless the intention is to have 'combative' or 'antagonistic' continuo, to obtain a stereophonic effect, as in "battenti" or "spezzati" cases. All these effects work wonderfully well when there are many continuo players.

4. While playing, the 'cellist should bear in mind not only the notes but also the figures written for the harpsichord: for example, a figure '2' could imply a *messa di voce* (a dissonant chord) which on its resolution to a '6' requires a *diminuendo*.

5. The keyboard player has the licence to simplify the harmony (leaving the dissonance to the soloist) or on the other hand to complicate matters with dissonances. Daube (1756): *"An elaborate accompaniment can add or remove dissonances indicated by the composer"*. C.P.E. Bach (1753) suggests "in a slow tempo, harmonise dissonances and their resolutions; in a medium tempo, only the dissonances; in a quick tempo, only the chord of resolution".

6. The same C.P.E. Bach writes that in very virtuosic passages it is fine for the harpsichord to play the smaller note values while the 'cello plays a simplification, or vice versa.

7. In recitatives there is a great freedom in the textural density. Saint-Lambert (1707): *"When accompanying a long recitative it is sometimes better to repeat the chords or, in contrast, sometimes to leave the soloist without accompaniment"*. We can also take great liberties with the placing of cadences. Let us look at these passages from a recitative from J.S. Bach's *St. Matthew Passion*. In bar 21 the cadence appears after the last word; however at bar 24 of the same recitative we see instead that the cadence overlaps with the last word:

8. The continuo can be 'coloured' by adopting different instruments, according to mood, the characters portrayed in the oratorio etc., and so maintaining interest by variety in the performance. C.P.E.Bach (1753): *The organ is indispensable in church music; the harpsichord in chamber music or recitatives"*.

And this leads us to....

Chapter 11: Instrumentation

IN THE BEGINNING THERE WAS....INSTRUMENTATION
The use of colour is a characteristic resource of the Baroque, ever since Monteverdi (in his opera 'Orfeo') specified, for the first time, the assortment of the orchestral accompaniment.

In the realm of infinite freedom encouraged by the Baroque we find choice of instrumental colour. An air for violin can be ceded to the oboe, the *flauto dolce*, (recorder), the transverse flute. And we have just seen how the continuo allows (requires!) these nuances. Remember that composers dived into these practices without hesitation: Bach took the concertos of Vivaldi and turned them into compositions for the organ, or recycled his own compositions with changes of instrumentation.

C. 'HOUSE SPECIALS'

C1. The role of the director: Gesture

It is interesting to discover that we do not come up against any great problems of gesture in baroque repertoire. There are not the brusque changes of tempo that we find in later periods, and the shape of the bars tends to fall within certain patterns. So, when should one beat time?

At the beginning: it is important to bear in mind the speed of the opening of each movement because, in contrast to other genres, an oratorio requires continuity. At the end: a simple *ritenuto* before the last note is enough, and subliminally it should hint at the speed of the next movement.

For the rest of the movement a continual beat is usually superfluous. The performers should be allowed plenty of freedom, with beating only where essential. This minimalist approach makes any gesture more meaningful, in order to add something new and enriching.

It is not necessary to beat time in *secco* recitative, as the natural fluidity and understanding between soloist and accompaniment is enough and renders gestures from the conductor redundant.

The only time it is necessary to revert to more elaborate gestures is in accompanied recitative, which has indeed to be conducted with great concentration because each section usually has its own rhythm. The *accompagnati* in Bach's *St. Matthew Passion* are particularly exigent in this way. The gesture involves not only tempo, but volume and articulation as well.

The gesture can also be linked to ornamentation: a conductor in the fortunate position of being able to rely on expert continuo players can indicate just with gestures who should enrich the musical texture and when.

In the end we could say that baroque music conducts itself with the brain, and a pencil (see chapter C5), rather than with hands or an 18th century baton.

C.2 The role of the director as teacher.

An oratorio is an extended work. It is important to be able to explain to the choir the different textual contexts, telling the overall story and the development of the various lines of the plot. This is even more necessary for the instrumentalists who usually only take part in the final rehearsals and cannot refer to the text.

It could be useful to copy the text of the choruses and solos into the orchestral parts, especially in the numerous passages where the voices and instruments share the same notes. These should reflect the sound of the text. As to the meaning, brief phrases or key-words can be used to indicate the character of each section to the instrumentalists (for example 'battle', or 'procession').

C.3 Relationship with the soloists.

An oratorio is a complex process, a mix of heterogeneous forces (choir, orchestra, soloists). As with the instruments, the soloists usually participate only in the final rehearsals. And so it can happen (with alarming frequency!) that a soloist has a different stylistic concept from that of the conductor (who presumably has already meticulously prepared a homogenous point of view with the choir, and in line with this has marked the orchestral parts – see section C.5).
This type of conflict of interest, or vision, often happened in the baroque era itself, and so we can celebrate this as a philological 'revival'!
In order to lessen this divergence it is essential to rehearse in detail with the soloists before they rehearse with the orchestra. Another solution, taken directly from Handel when directing his own concerts, is to include the soloists in the choral fabric, which would promote stylistic consistency and make for a more democratic performance.

C.4 Cuts

IN THE BEGINNING THERE WERE....CUTS
To gorge excessively can provoke indigestion. One should restrict the diet so as not to lose the attention of the listeners.

The large baroque works (Oratorios, Passions) are of a length which we are no longer accustomed to today. Indeed we are told that in the intervals between the acts of his longest oratorios, Handel improvised on the harpsichord or inserted his *Concerti Grossi*, in musical evenings that lasted 5 or 6 hours!
To adapt these colossal works to the frenetic tempo of today we suggest making certain cuts. This does not go against the spirit of that time: in several cases Handel himself has left differing versions of the same work, adding or removing movements according to the occasion and available soloists. For example, when the famous countertenor Giovanni Carestini was engaged for the second performance of *Athalia*, Handel reworked the entire oratorio, cutting certain numbers in order to insert new arias in Italian written expressly for the new protagonist.
And so we see that the flexibility of approach that we have mentioned before touches every aspect. And remember that too excessive a respect for the score would appear to be bordering on indifference in the eyes of someone from that period, and a symptom of an inability to adapt the work to different circumstances.
What criteria can we use in this delicate surgical procedure? AVOID BORING the audience by maintaining an appropriate variety of colour; but WITHOUT compromising the narrative logic, and respecting an acceptable sequence of key relationships.
CS: Handelian writing was such that all the soloists should participate in an oratorio in equal manner. So, if deciding to make cuts one would do well to respect this balance according to the reduced scale of the work; for instance how to judge the right amount of instrumental numbers (which were used as '*intermezzi*'), recitatives (boring for a modern audience) and choruses (always powerful and captivating even for today's listeners).

In the specific case of the oratorio *Judas Maccabeus*, on which we will base the examples in this book, we are proposing ONE of the possible feasible shortenings, cutting the following numbers:
Recitative *"To Heaven's..."*; Aria *"O liberty..."*; Aria *"Come, ever-smiling liberty"*; Recitative *"Ambition!...*; Aria *"No unhallow'd desire"*; Recitative *"O Judas"*; Recitative *"Haste we..."*; Chorus *"Hear us, O Lord"*; Recitative *"Victorius hero"*; Aria *"So rapid thy couse is"*; Recitativo *"Well may hope..."*; Duet and chorus *"Sion now her head..."*; Recitative *"O let eternal honours..."*; Aria *"From mighty Kings..."*; Recitative *"Again to heart..."*.

C.5 Orchestral material

First of all, we would suggest the avoidance of editions that give directions for interpretation. In the Baroque period these indications were not given in the score. This would suggest that any such markings found in the score are most probably distinctly 18th century.
However, the conductor should mark up the instrumental parts in accordance with HIS interpretation. For economic reasons, the preparation of an oratorio usually can rely on only a few rehearsals, and marking the general shape of the desired interpretation in the parts in advance will save a lot of time. Work with the pencil (as we said earlier, the director's principal instrument) can prevent a great deal of problems, but not all. During a full rehearsal I will probably lose around 15% of my markings....however, the remaining 85% of the advance markings will make for a very efficient rehearsal, and will greatly deepen my preparative study of the work (Bach copied in minute detail Vivaldi's Concerti in his efforts to learn; Mozart dedicated himself to similar tasks...so we must always bear in mind that we will only discover all the hidden treasures by studying every single note!).
With my 'pencil-chisel' I can hint at macro- and micro-dynamics in detail with signs such as these (this example taken from Telemann's *Wassermusik*):

using the conventional signs of *diminuendo*, *crescendo*, *staccato* (see Section B.2, point 3); an arrow to show that a note is joined to the next which belongs to a new phrase; the sign 'N.A.' (no accent) and/or brackets to show the lightening of a note that falls on a strong beat, as a contrast to the common tendency of accenting them emphatically.
I leave, instead, the overall macro dynamic to the inspiration of the moment (actually, an unexpected change in texture can sometimes be needed to maintain the interest of the audience, or even of the musicians themselves!).

For the subtle Agogic ebb and flow, I could use the following signs:

The 'coroncina' (upside-down pause) would indicate a slight *tenuto* effect (see Section B.4, point 4), while the 'serpentello' would indicate small *rubati* in the moving quavers, to avoid monotony.

C.6 Placing and the stage

We are not obliged to conform to the traditional orchestral placing (orchestra sitting in front with the choir standing behind). This formation, which was born out of the age-old class battle between instrumentalists and choristers, among other things, does not entirely correspond with acoustical logic, which would imply that the chorus hears the sound of the orchestra through the players' backs. This would make it much harder for the singers to keep in tune than for the players. We could position the choir seated in front of the orchestra....or mix them with the orchestra: for example, first violin/a soprano, second violin/an alto, viola/a tenor, cello/a bass. Using this pattern for the first row, we could arrange the second row in mirror image the opposite way...and so on for further rows.
Other small variants: we could scatter just the continuo instruments among the choir; or we could divide just the sopranos into two groups, placing them either side of the stage.
Some conductors suggest moving the choir around during a performance, and with some success. For example, during a Passion the choir could move to different positions according to their role (chorale/chorus/crowd). Any one of these combinations would be more creative than the traditional placing, and could make for an arresting stereo effect.
Clearly all of this places a greater (and welcome!) responsibility on the individual chorister, and practically eliminates the semaphore gesticulations of the conductor because it makes it impossible to give 'topografical' gestures for the entrances of various sections.

C.7 The structure of the concert

Because an oratorio is a long work, with a complicated storyline, often in a foreign language, it can be helpful to an audience to have some kind of clean and clear commentary to illustrate the plot.
This 'guide' could take various forms:
a.   By telling the story on a day before the concert, and using just choir, soloists and a keyboard, and illustrating it with musical fragments.
b.   During the concert, a speaker could explain the plot briefly at the beginning of each of the (usually) three acts of the oratorio. To create an appropriate atmosphere, a gentle musical background could be provided (a baroque composition for harpsichord or lute, or an improvisation in baroque style).

c.   During the concert there could be projected subtitles, which could include images that evoke the story.

C.8 For Dessert...the tympani.

The dynamics of those instruments considered the most 'noisy' (tympani, trumpets, horns) are often neglected, when instead they should be object of detailed musical attention.

When the trumpets or horns don't have a virtuoso melodic function but merely fulfill the role of a fanfare, often together with the tympani, their dynamics should be detailed with great care, thereby obtaining a much more intense interpretation. We have used the term "dessert" in the sense of proposing 'a little extra', because even though the tympani part is often not indicated in the score, the presence of trumpets can allow for their addition 'ex novo' as part of the fanfare. When doing this we would advise taking inspiration from Handel's oratorios, where we often come across an attractive heterophony between trumpets and drums, as we see in this example from *Israel in Egypt*:

D. JUDAS MACCABEUS:
221 NOTATED EXAMPLES

Now let us consider a representative oratorio, *Judas Maccabeus*, to view in greater detail the criteria suggested in the previous sections. We will deal with various different scenarios, which, as we have already mentioned on numerous occasions, will afford our interpretation much more choice. And so we will indicate what is more a concoction of possible outcomes than a recipe of absolute truth.

We have selected 221 examples, relating them wherever possible to the criteria as suggested in the previous pages.

Moreover, as a complement to this book, we also recommend a live recording of a performance of *Judas Maccabeus*, given on 14th October 2012 in the ATE Theatre in Santa Fe, Argentina, performed by the *Orquesta Barroca del Suquía* (director Manfred Kraemer) and the Coro Polifónico Provincial de Santa Fe, conducted by Sergio Siminovich.

This live recording was not made with this book in mind because we were not thinking of an audio supplement to the text. But as we have the luck to have recorded the concert, the musical material seems to be a useful addition to the academic text.

A few words about the performers:

The *Coro Polifónico Provincial de Santa Fe* and the *Orquesta Barroca del Suquía* are professional groups, and Manfred Kraemer is one of the most important performers of baroque music internationally.

Listening carefully to this version of *Judas Maccabeus* will reveal to what extent these talented performers follow the criteria outlined in this book, and also how much they (legitimately!) depart from the inevitable limits of such patterns.

In this way you will also realize that no book is able to summarise every valid interpretation, and so we hope you will exercise generosity in excusing the gaps in our "Baroque Possibilities".

Overture, **First Part.**

1. A Baroque *Overture* generally requires a staccato articulation with a very
    pointed rhythm (double-dotted, as shown in various treatises, to bring to
    the audience's attention that the piece is beginning!).

2. Apply *messa di voce*, so that the prolonged *A* of the violins and oboes creates
    a dissonance with the *Eflat-C* chord, which then resolves, with a light agogic
    lengthening suggested by the embellishment in the second bar [Chapter 4,
    point 11].

3. As in bars 4 to 5, we have a harmonic resolution in bars 6 to 7 from the
    dominant to the tonic. So begin these bars with a *diminuendo*. Similarly, in
    bars 9, 11, 13 and 15, always look to avoid the danger of symmetry [Chapter
    4, point 8].

4. The *F sharp* in bar 9 is just as much the end of a phrase as the beginning of
    another one. And so the *diminuendo* is followed by a *crescendo*.

5.   There is a dissonance in bar 10: cultivate this by accentuating the bass.

6.   The passage for First Violin is normally elegantly embellished in this way (*tirata*):

7.   Melodic climax, underlined with a small accent.

8.   The phrase ends in bar 13. In this case it is treated as a half-cadence to the dominant.

9.   As in example 6 we suggest that the *ripieno* be treated the same way (*tirata*).

10. We have at least two possible options for the *da capo* of the first part of the
     Overture:
     a.   Repeat with only oboe, one cello and harpsichord.
     b.   Repeat with only one violin, one cello and harpsichord, with the
          ornamentation that we suggest for both string instruments.

Overture, Second Part – *Allegro*

11.   A repeated note usually implies a *crescendo*, in this instance for two bars as an upbeat, as if it were in 6/8 [Chapter 4, point 14].

We place a big bar line before the *D*, to show that this is the true point of arrival [Chapter 4' point 13].

12.   In accordance with our view of **Articulation** [Chapter 5, point 3], the quavers should be *staccato*.

13.   A small gap before the accent is implied in the trill [Chapter 5, point 1].

14.   Bridge of two bars *legato*, and so quite free rhythmically [**Agogics**, Chapter 7, point 6].

15.   Characterise the melismatic quavers by separating the mini-phrases of a leap of a third, and underline this with a gentle *diminuendo* before the leap (rather like applying the brakes before changing down a gear)) [Chapter 4, point 7].

16. There is a hemiola (bars of 3/4 in a context of 3/8) the form of a typical cadence. It acts as a punctuation mark, which we can mark in the instrumental parts (with a 3/4 sign), and we will conduct it that way.

    Avoid an accent on the third quaver (the second beat of the hemiola), emphasizing instead the fifth quaver (the third beat of the hemiola), which corresponds to the expressive accent in a trill (for example, as seen in the well known frottola "L'Amor Donna ch'io ti porto"…).

17. A small pause (which we have called the 'coroncina') [Chapter 7, point 4] before the bridge which precedes the important *Tutti* entrance in bar 107, like a film camera briefly holding a zoomed-in image before opening out into a panorama.

18. A rhetorical accent on the highest note of the phrase, remaining for an instant in this *climax*, like a victory cry.

19. Change to *piano* for a brief five-bar coda.

20. Our first cut: to shorten the Overture and begin the narrative of the oratorio, we can cut the *Lentamente* section and go directly to bar 162.

Act 1 – Chorus *"Mourn, ye afflicted children"*

21. The **Articulation** of this number requires separate quavers, as they correspond to the syllables of the chorus. [Chapter 5, point 3].

22. An almost '*Schumannian*' chord which should be emphasized with a slight agogic inflexion (reinforced by the fact that the dissonance *E flat-B natural* is not prepared).

23. The orchestra must get out of the way with an timely *diminuendo* to allow for the chorus entry.

24. The text suggests *rubato* in the crotchets. There are various possibilities, the object being to avoid overall tedium.

25. The soprano note should end with the contraltos.

26. Accent the most important and dramatic note of the syllable "san-" as much with rhythmic delays (agogics) as with dynamics.

27. Enunciate the three qualities of the leader Mattatia, "*hero, father, friend*" with special emphasis.

28. Bring out the heterophony between the violins and the bass.

29. Hesitate for a moment agogically before the definitive word *"more"*, as if to delay the announcement of such terrible news.

B. friend, and fa - ther is no more,

And define the articulation of the bass part to distinguish between monosyllables and bi-syllables.

30. Handel sometimes used this expedient (see *Acis and Galatea*, *Belshazzar*, *Trauer Ode*): leave the choir unaccompanied when speaking of death, as if the instruments were incapable of alluding to such an extreme subject, and only the human voice were able to describe the existential angst.

S. is no more:

A. is no more:

T. is no more:

B. is no more:

31. Lighten the notes without syllables, making them *piano* and *legato* [Chapter 5, point 3].

Ob. I.II.

Vl. I.

Vl. II.

Vla

S. sol - - emn

A. mourn in sol - emn

T. sol - - emn

B. sol - - emn

B.C.

32. This typical ending contains what is also known as the *"Purcellian dissonance"*: that of the *B natural* against the *C*. Emphasise it and enjoy it.

Recitative *"Well may your sorrows"*

33. Here we meet the first recitative of the oratorio. Recitatives usually are the less attractive part for the audience (and for the singers!). The difficulties of language, when it is a foreign one, and the want of a melody can dissipate their attention.

A good singer approaches a recitative as if telling a story, with inflexions more spoken than sung. It is a great help to vary the speed and to give the phrases direction, ignoring some of the rests.

Similarly a good continuo player varies the texture [Chapter 10, point 2], as one might in a piano bar, or recalling the keyboard style of silent cinema accompaniment.

Any creative seasoning will help to achieve the required fluidity. The length of the chords should also be varied: long, sustained chords are not always necessary.

For example, we can differentiate the chords by lengthening the dominant and shortening the tonic [as in Chapter 4, point 8].

To provide lots of colour, change instrument according to the character that is singing, which will require a careful assignment of roles.

Duet *"From this dread scene"*

34. The real bar line for the First Violin is just before bar 2 [Chapter 4, point 13] and just before bar 3 for the Second Violin.

35. The first phrase of the soloist expresses two ideas ["Affetti" see Appendix 1], one per bar. We can therefore incorporate these easily into the Violin figure.

From this   dread   scene,   these   ad - verse   pow'rs,

36. Obligatory trill [Chapter 9, point 1]. Ideally, the necessary *appoggiatura* (*B flat*) should not sweeten the jarring between the two Violins.

37. In the Violins, bar 14 can be performed in two ways: with a *diminuendo* in the bouncing of the repeated notes, or with a *crescendo* which continues until the climactic *E flat* of the soloist, together with a dramatic leap of a ninth.

ad - verse   pow'rs,   Ah!

38. To evoke the 'smoky' effect of the text we can combine *legato* with a tired, almost indolent, atmosphere.

39. Here is an ideal place for a *cadenza* for both soloists, or, if no *cadenza*, for a decisive *Adagio* to allow for a beautiful union of the two voices.

Chorus *"For Sion lamentation make"*

40. As Schweitzer [1955] pointed out so clearly [see Appendix 1], the rhythm of
     the continuo represents funeral bells.

41. By reading the figuring of the continuo, the 'cellist will know where to
     crescendo and *diminuendo*. A more complex figuring creates a more
     dissonant texture, and so the volume should increase accordingly.

42. Don't put the 's' on the rest [Chapter 8, point 5].

43. The third beat of bar 12 works as an expressive climax: the violins act as a bridge towards bar 13 of the alto and tenor, which begins with an accent followed by an expressive agogic delay, while the violins lighten the texture to leave space for the chorus.

44. Accent the dissonance in the soprano part (4-3). It is the most commonly occurring musical dissonance, from Palestrina to pop, and correctly emphasized never loses its effect.

45. The alto voice, which will create a similar dissonance (4-3), links the upbeat
     to bar 28 more than the other voices with a significant *crescendo*, like a
     'trailer' announcing the dissonance.

Aria *"Pious orgies"*

46. A flexible *rubato* in the violins, as if disdaining the structured stability of the
     first three beats of the viola and continuo.

47. Basic dynamic formula [Chapter 5, point 5] with its three typical elements:
     upbeat, accent and weak syllable (feminine ending, as in the pattern "ba-
     roc-co").

48. Articulation of the continuo: detached step [Chapter 5, point 2].

49. A gap (*caesura*) before the expressive noun [Chapter 5, point 2].

De - cent sor- row,__

50. The 'basic formula' appears once more.

move His pi-ty, His pi - ty

51. Ornamentation implied, as in examples 6 and 9.

sor- row,   decent

52. It is interesting to connect the third beat to the fourth, in order to underline the tension in the harmony, and in this way avoid symmetrical shape.

53. A rest filled with tension. In this way we learn to distinguish between empty rests and rests that are "full".

Chorus "*O father, whose almighty power*"

54. The 'basic formula' is back, this time with clear articulation: a short upbeat underlines the following accent.

55. A big *diminuendo* in the downwards octave leap, like a bounce, an echo.

56. A good example of dissimilarity: here the choral text needs a different articulation to that of the string *incipit* (example 54). There being no doubling by the instruments we can allow this 'irregularity', and so perhaps adding to the mystical character of unaccompanied chorus or to the heterogeneity that appears in so many aspects of the Baroque, and emphasizing the eloquence of the words in bar 13.

57. A *melisma* that merits close attention, with dynamic hairpins that clearly indicate the separation of phrases.

58. The dotted crotchet in the second violin and continuo functions as a bridge to the choral entry, and so needs a *crescendo*, which surmounts the leap of a 7th.

59. Avoid regular accents on each bar [Chapter 4, point 13], lightening *"Thy"*.

60. The bridging phrase in the second violins begins on the second quaver,
implying a lightening of the first quaver of bar 33 (the harmonic resolution
to the tonic).

61. The *swing* of the fugal theme is obtained by emphasizing the consonants
[Chapter 8, point 1]. In general, *staccato* is used less often for the choir than
for the orchestra, but this would be a good moment to suggest a bright and
incisive *staccato*.

At bar 39, we find a weaker syllable on "*-quer*", and at bar 40 from the
second quaver a busy bridge in the continuo part.

62. Carefully lighten the contralto notes that are on the one syllable, especially as it is a rising melodic shape and is doubled by the viola and second violin.

63. In bar 49, the last three quavers of the first violins are a linking passage, so play them *"alla corda"* (a *staccato* would evoke the wobbling of a rather unstable bridge).

64. A *crescendo* for the modulation:

65. The tenor has an octave leap on a weak syllable to disguise parallel fifths with the bass part. Therefore be very careful to lighten this rather banal and functional upper *F*.

66. Instead, underline the *E flat* in the tenor part (an unprepared 7th) to give prominence and character to such an epic moment.

Accompanied recitative *"I feel the deity within"*

67. The notation of the rhythm in this period implies a convention: the writing was plain, but the execution of these rhythms was always double-dotted (a good example of the spirit as opposed to the letter - one might say of the literature as opposed to the literal).

68. Here the cadence in the strings is delayed until after the third beat of the soloist [Chapter 10, point 7].

69. At the end of bar 15 shorten the note in the strings. It should be no longer than 2 beats.

Chorus and solo "Arm, arm ye brave"

70. Rhythmic freedom when the continuo stops ("when the cat's away the mice will play…").

In bar 2, lean on the top note, as a kind of victory. Don't succumb to the violinist's usual panic in these passages, with a rather suspect *diminuendo*.

71. Make the phrase from the last quaver of bar 3 *legato* as a surprise after so much *staccato*.

72. To make up for its lack of contrapuntal interest the unison needs character and volume, so as not to sound empty and redundant.

73. Don't hit the final notes of the half-cadence in bar 8.

74. Although the string parts progress by steps, the cadence needs separated chords at the change of harmony from 6-4 to 5-3.

75. The almost 'hollywoodian' crescendo in the first violins needs to be played *alla corda*, making its mark also on the second violins and violas.

76. Handel suggests a colourful instrumentation (the bassoon doubles the soloist, and later appears within the woodwind trio). Don't let this detail of colour pass unnoticed.

77. A *crescendo* in the short instrumental bridging passages where the emphatic soloist is silent.

78. Once again, the first violin phrase should be subdivided in accordance with the leap and change of direction of the melody [Chapter 4, point 7].

79. The length of the accents can be varied agogically to coincide with the expressive leaps [Chapter 7, point 4], with eloquent words.

80. The *B natural* dominates obsessively for three bars during the little list sung by the soloist (*"nation"*, *"religion"*, *"laws"*) until reaching the *C* (on *"Almighty"*).

81. The climax comes on the name of God ("*Jehovah*"), on the high *E*.

82. The rhythm describes a gallop.

83. *Crescendo* during the last quavers as the harmonic rhythm increases its speed (ultimately to more than one chord per bar).

84. Rhetorically, the name of the protagonist is evoked three times, as in traditional liturgical invocations. The dactyl violin rhythm is brought to the fore with an accent on each beat.

85. To give the impression of a tumultuous crowd (like the turbe in the Passions) the voices follow one another in a *stretto*, which should be indicated with an accent on every entrance. Avoid an accent on the soprano *E* at bar 103, as it does not have its own syllable.

86.   We can place the verb in relief by preceding it with a small *ceasura*.

87.   A typical conclusion (very often seen in Bach), with an expansion of the basic harmony (on the tonic with a seventh in the continuo) as if to announce the end.

Aria *"Call forth thy pow'rs"*

88. To give shape to these phrases put the last note of the first scale in
    parentheses. The semi-quavers should be alla corda and the quavers *staccato*,
    for three good reasons: their longer note-value, the leaps, and the implicit
    change of harmony $^6/_4$ - $^5/_3$.

89. Play the figure in bar 4 as a fanfare, corresponding to the war-like soloist,
    and put rhetorical accents on the syllable *"con-"* in bars 6 and 7.

    The outcome of war is always uncertain: which is why the *melismas* are so
    sinuous, requiring mastery of the Art of the Melisma.

90. At the soloist's pause the instruments should *crescendo*.

91. Now is the moment to stop this cascade of notes. We can do this at any point in bar 29. Each option has its own attraction. The tenor's *A sharp* (bar 29) can be held, as a proud trophy.

Duet *"Come ever-smiling liberty"*

92. In a three-quaver figure the second quaver often has no syllable of its own, and so should lighten off.

93. There is a wonderful chord in bar 11 which is quite advanced for baroque musical language. Treating it as a delicate moment of intimacy we can emphasise this by stretching its length a little. We can also prolong the note before the soloist's fast semiquavers.

94. Tension on the dominant and release on the tonic.

95. Careful articulation of the violins should not hinder the feeling of forward movement.

96. Don't spoil the dance-like elegance of this number by accenting the high crotchets, but the quavers that preceed them instead.

Chorus *"Lead on"*

97. The strings should hammer their chords to 'wake up' the audience after the calm duet.

98. Alternate the accents where the protagonist is named.

99. A nice effect could be achieved by joining the first beat to the second, marking a link across the comma with an expressive arrow.

Semi-chorus *"Disdainful of Danger"*

100. General articulation: semiquavers alla corda, especially when repeating notes; quavers *staccato* [Chapter 5, point 3]. As in many instances in triple time, group as if in ⁶/₈.

Violino I.

Violino II.

101. A tiny gap before the first note of the cadence, like a mini-pause before announcing a conclusion.

Vl.I.

Vl.II.

Vla.

B.C.

102. The strings emerge from so many bars of merely doubling to dominate, passing from background to subject.

Vl. I.

Vl. II.

Vla.

A.

dain-ful,we'll rush on the foe,   That Thy

T.

dain-ful,we'll rush on the foe,   That Thy

B.

dain-ful,we'll rush on the foe,   That Thy

B.C.

103. A change of mood, here describing the act of kneeling, prostrate before the divine power.

104. Because of the instrumental writing, we run the risk of emphasizing a *hemiola* that does not exist, and which is at odds with the accents in the chorus parts.

105. Act I ends here. To give the good sense of an ending we suggest a "Little Reprise", often used in the Baroque, by repeating the last three bars piano, as a fading echo.

Act 2 – Chorus *"Fallen is the foe"*

106. The phrasing of this very long *melisma* needs intelligence and a busy pencil (otherwise the instrumentalists will approach it with a constant, inflexible *mf*).

107. Where the continuo is silent the linking phrases in the violins are always energetic. Here they maintain the structure more as beams in the roof than as the foundation.

108. At bar 13, choral onomatopoeia. The strings must imitate this style of attack but without obscuring the explosive "*F*" that precedes the note. At bar 15, unify the phrasing of the choir and the strings, slurring the quavers that don't have their own syllable.

109. The soprano high note has the function of great emphasis.

110. Pay great attention to this passage, putting all the notes that do not have their own syllable in parentheses. But being careful not to leave out the final "*s*"s – an important refinement.

111. Tricky bars: the phrasing of the mainly syllabic tenor part is simple; the bass part is as in the previous example. The alto part is the most difficult as it is almost without syllables: a good phrasing would grow towards the plaintively expressive *B flat*, without giving it an accent.

112. The rhetorical use of the sung "*f*" sound should create....a sensation of terror (judiciously amplified by the *piano* dynamic, almost whispered).

113. A slight *ritenuto* on the fifth quaver before the thematic figure, to clarify
     the structure by slowing the previous section and announcing the following
     one.

114. A rhetorical, stabbing repetition of the verb.

115. Lengthening the fourth beat creates a sense of suspense before the finale, and without juggling with the continuo, which is silent for this upbeat.

Duet and Chorus *"Hail, Judea, happy land"*

116. The chords change from tonic to dominant and back to the tonic in quick succession, like a drum. Treat them like karate-chops as a confident affirmation, as if delineating territorial boundaries. At bar 2 we reach the highest note: an elegant climax without a rustic accent, with a small agogic delay, owing to the change of direction in the melody.

117. The last three violin quavers are a bridging point: play *alla corda* (see example 14).

118. The third beat of bar 54 is as much an ending as a new beginning (see example 4). The effect is that of bringing down the curtain and a change of scene.

Aria *"How vain is man who boasts in fight"*

119. Do not accent the low note, because the dactyl rhythm (see example 84) implies an accent with a *diminuendo* on the following two notes.

Violino I. II.

120. Play as if two voices, as in compositions for one melody instrument (a *Fantasia* by Telemann or a Bach *Partita*).

Violino I. II.

121. Do not accent the downward interval (see example 119).

Vl. I. II.

B.C.

122. Make sure that these bars are not rhythmically mechanical by placing a caesura before the last quaver of bar 39 and before the third beat of bar 41.

Vl. I. II.

B.C.

How

123. The obsessive repeating note (firstly in the *continuo*, then in the violins)
describes very eloquently the word *"fight"*.

124. The second part of this aria hints at a change of colour: so let us move from
the harpsichord to the theorbo.

Solo and Chorus *"Ah! Wretched Israel"*

125. Handel indicates *"solo cello"*. A harmony instrument (theorbo or organ) should only join in at the point where the bass figuring appears at bar 6. This device can be adopted in other similar places, with very effective results. The cello should join the semiquaver to the crotchet, as in the soprano text. This kind of articulation indicates *resistance*. Slurring the first two notes instead would suggest *resignation*.

126. Articulate bar 33 by joining the first two crotchets.

127. Climax on the 4-3 dissonance, the first dissonance of the piece, up until now full of serene modal accord.

128. We illustrate the downward interval on *"fall'n"* with a subito *piano*, like a nasty surprise, underlined by the continuo seventh.

129. Bar 60 could be seen as suspended, an echo frozen in time.

130. In this concise moment of beauty, we can add the passing note and the trill to the first violin.

131. An expressive upbeat in the viola and second violin parts, raising their function from mere *ripieno* to create a bridge.

132. Coroncina' on the bar line between bars 102 and 103, to establish a clear shape: change of text...change of scene.

133. We encounter the most dramatic chord in the Baroque; the diminished seventh (it appears in the Passions of Bach when alluding to Judas Iscariot or Barabbas).

We deal with this aria in greater depth in Appendix E.2

Aria *"The Lord worketh wonders"*

134. Having a function that is merely melodic (decorative) rather than harmonic (cadential), the trill does not need a too long an *appoggiatura*. We would suggest that the true barline, as sometimes happens in Telemann and Vivaldi, corresponds to the third beat.

135. We suggest a varied articulation:

It is very difficult to phrase the long *melismas* in this aria. It could be the subject of an exam in an advanced study in….Melismas!

136. The high *D* is a climax which deserves to be stressed, in contrast to what we have already seen for many other *melismas* [Chapter 4, point 9], to illustrate clearly the word *"raise"*.

137. The *melisma* in bar 26 is much harder to shape than that in bar 24, in which we could rely on the help of leaps of a fourth, like milestones along the road.

glo -   ry,   His glo -

138. Instead, we suggest not accenting the violin *D sharp*, as the melismatic phrase begins on the following note.

Vl.I.II.

139. Accent the low notes where the harmony changes, like the supporting notes in a *Partita* for solo violin.

Vl. I.II.

B.C.

140. Change of mood ("affetto"); as the text changes so we find calmer note values, and a sixth as an unprepared dissonant cadence. The quavers that follow need an expressive *portato*.

Vl.I.II.

fear-ful in praise,   is   fear - ful in praise,

B.C.

Solo and Chorus *"Sound an alarm"*

141. Every quaver is a pulsation (so, *staccato*) and we also have frequent changes of harmony.

142. In the agogic style as mentioned in example 80, with the note E as an obsessive ground.

143. Articulate as a typical *Gigue*:

with a *diminuendo* on the second quaver of each group (an almost tyrolean "yodel" effect), followed by an anxious *crescendo* on the following upbeats formed of two notes each with their own syllable.

144. Difficult phrasing, because it is in reiterative form. It needs to be played with contrasting dynamics.

145. Change of mood, together with a change of metrical emphasis.

146. The way that *"justice"* and *"courage"* alternate in height would seem to indicate that they are equally important.

147. A rhetorical pause, as if seeing the troops in the distance.

Sound an a-larm

148. Here we encounter a meta-linguistic device of an unprepared seventh in the soprano line, which forces us to *"hear"*.

We hear, we hear, we

We hear, we hear, we

We hear, we hear, we

We hear, we hear, we

149. *"Pleasing"* is on the more peaceful subdominant chord, characteristic of refreshing oases. In contrast, *"Dreadful"* is on a brusquer chord, that of the sharpened sixth.

150. The violin figure in bars 41 and 42 is as much about the word *"follow"* as it is about the discharging of an arquebus (see *"The trumpet's loud clangour"* in Handel's *Ode to Saint Cecilia*, bar 66).

151. The first uttering of the word *"conquest"* is a blunt tonic-dominant, as if imitating tympani.

152. The chordal sequence of sevenths suggests that an elegant *"fall"* is not necessarily conclusive.

153. An old self-help book (Carnegie 1936) teaches us that the word most welcome to our ears is…our own name! Here the highest soprano note (top A, which will only appear once more in the whole oratorio) is on the word "*we*".

Recitative *"Enough: to Heav'n we leave the rest"*

154. The modulating note (*B flat* at bar 4) underlines the word "*divide*", and announces the change of function of the chord on C.

155. The *B flat* (diminished seventh, bar 11) refers retrospectively to the word "*profanation*".

Aria *"With pious hearts"*

156. The slurs across the beat (very Vivaldian) allude to hesitation or to pleading.

157. We can make an expressive accent....by subtraction [Chapter 4, point 9], choosing to keep the high note very light (the tyrolean yodel effect already mentioned in example 143). It is much more attractive than to hit every high note willy nilly.

158. We can delay on the trill: this will capture attention and trigger suspense, as with so many other upbeats.

159. An expressive slur at bar 22 in the violins (it would have much less force were the notes only to be *E-D-C-E-D-C*, without the expressive leap to the *F*).

160. Similarly, *F-D-A* is much more expressive than *F-G-A*. Questioning the composer's motives for every note that he chooses is an excellent exercise in developing interpretation.

161. The word *"God"* involves a categorical unison. What is more, it features an unusual chord of the eleventh.

We see a similar moment in *Messiah*, in the chorus *"For unto us a child is born"*.

Aria *"Wise men, flattering, may deceive us"*

162. The first bars suggest a light articulation, like a Minuet. This mood changes in bars 5 – 8.

A well-distributed asymmetry will avoid an accent on every bar. To this end the soloist's text could be a great help.

Wise men,___ flat - t'ring, may de - - ceive us With their vain ___ mys - te - rious ___ art,

Duet and Chorus *"We never will bow down "*

163. The continuo needs to be figured very carefully as the harmony could change in every bar… or every quaver! There are various possibilities:

a) 5/3 ____ 7
b) 5/3 ____ 6 ____ 6 7

164. An unusual bridging passage, which almost disappears in a delicate
diminuendo, as if the violins are giving the impression that they would like
to leave the stage for a little while.

165. We could risk a different semantic weight for every single word of the phrase
"but ever worship Israel's God": uncertainty/eternity/devotion/instability/
stability.

166. Here some 'structural licence' would be allowed so as not to lose continuity by combining bars 87 and 88. We know that this often happened to join successive movements.

CORO - "We never, never will bow down"

167. If we avoid a breath in the tenors and basses at the join (bar 114) we create more tension. An arrow could be used to indicate this. The same at bar 123 for the sopranos and altos.

168. The chord on the word *"God"* is unusual, like God himself, to our constant amazement... for "He is the One who is", transcending human understanding.

169. A difficult *melisma* which betrays its instrumental origin (Corelli). It should be played with intelligence and refinement, its great length and range fortunately helped by the support of the violins (in contrast to the kilometric length of the *melisma* in *Fecit potentiam* from Bach's *Magnificat*, which cannot rely on such support).

170. From bar 173 we can adopt an instrumental accentuation (as in a Renaissance *bicinium*), leaning on the long, high note.

171. The unexpected high A depicts amazement in the face of God.

(musical notation)

S. lone, and God a - lone, we

A. lone, and God a - lone, we

T. lone, and God a - lone, we

B. lone, and God a - lone, we

B.C.

Act 3 – Aria *"Father of Heaven"*

172. The last three quavers mirror the familiar horn call over a fifth: they should be played *staccato*.

(musical notation)

Violino I.

Violino II.

Viola

Bassi

173. *Rubato* bridge over the third and fourth beats, using the delay to take advantage of the 'magnetic' effect of the dotted notes.

(musical notation)

Violino I.

Violino II.

Viola

Bassi

174. Do not accent the second *C*, as in 18th century practices (or renaissance polyrhythmia, as mentioned in example 170), but rather the preceeding quaver.

Vl. I.

175. Dynamics (*crescendo-diminuendo*) suggested by the different harmonic tensions.

Vl. I.

Vl. II.

Vla

B.C.

176. Transport of ecstasy, in free *tempo*. Quantz suggests that in this kind of passage, or in a soloistic cadenza, the audience should be surprised by an unexpectedly long breath. In this example, lengthen the minim *ad libitum*.

Fa - ther of Heav'n,

177. Emphasise the key-word *"Thy"*.

Vl. I.

Vl. II.

Vla

Fa - ther of Heav'n! from Thy e - ter - nal throne, from

B.C.

178. The final upbeat of bar 36 is probably the most beautiful phrase in the oratorio, reaching the heights. Identifying the moments of greatest beauty is fundamental in achieving an overall vision, and to conducting with involvement.

179. For a seductive effect, prolong the final note of bar 63, joining it to the beginning of bar 64.

Recitative *"O grant it, Heaven"*

180. Improvise a 'fanfare' with the continuo, emphasizing the word *"war"*.

Aria *"So shall the lute and harp awake"*

181. Great challenge: phrase the intricate violin *melisma*.

182. Do not accent the fifth note of the intricate violin *melisma*. It is a repetition of the first note and so carries no new information. It closes the circle with a bounce back to that first note.

183. Quantz suggests leaving out a note if there is not enough breath for such a long phrase. In this case, leave out the second note of bar 23 to breathe there.

184. A typical example of phrasing a *melisma* in a 5+3 pattern.

185. Here, instead, the phrasing will be 6+2 (it would have been 5+3 were the opening notes *C-B-C-D C-A-B-C*).

186. A splendid moment because the soloist can show off with a cadenza that demonstrates his strengths (extension or volume or breath control or imaginative ornamentation…as well as high theatricality).

Chorus *"See, the conqu'ring hero comes"*

187. A very simple piece to teach the choir because it systematically presents a note without a syllable, a strong syllable and a weak syllable. It is the best known choral piece by Handel after the *Halleluyah* chorus. Handel himself said "It is not my best piece, but it will certainly be the most famous!".

Solo and Chorus *"Sing unto God"*

188. Once more we are faced with the challenge of phrasing a sinuous melisma intelligently.

189. Rich words of import (*"high"*, *"crown"*, *"conquest"*), well set by Handel.

In the continuo at bar 10, do not accent the quaver that follows semiquaver (a deplorable habit…almost '*newtonian*'), because it is a moment of relaxation and consonance and not a cathartic release.

190. We would suggest that the first trumpet consider the *D* in bar 23 as the upbeat to the new phrase, imitated a little later by the other two trumpets.

191. The chorus altos, in the comfortable part of the voice, should imitate the brilliant sound of trumpets (with a full *A*).

192. A delightful bridging passage in the violins, worthy of emphasis.

193. The short note-values of the trumpets and timpani at the close of bar 50
     have the percussive and energizing function mentioned in Chapter 8, like a
     vigorous and impressive bridge.

194. Here is a lovely Joke by Handel: the rhythmic energy of bars 50 and 51 usually causes an instrumentalist or chorus member to forget to observe the full length of the rest before bar 52. We find this with many ensembles, amateur or professional…Handel probably smiles to himself every time this mistake happens…seeing as the text says *"With unmeasured praise"*!

195. A very slight accent on the brightest trumpet note: the high *D* (almost a syncopated jazz effect).

196. A similar case to example 193.

197. The finale can be even more brilliant, with this sort of fanfare shape:

Here (elaborated *ad hoc*) we are assuming that the *tutti* resolves in the third bar and that the fanfare prolongs the resolution with its exposed rhythmic figures, as we see in other compositions by Handel, for instance *Israel in Egypt*

Or in *Joshua*:

Aria *"With honour let desert be crowned"*

198. Unexpectedly modal chords. Handel generally used these colours to convey an archaic feel, evoking Old Testament times.

199. Evidently the word *"desert"* doesn't need instruments…

Chorus *"To our great God"*

200. The pronunciation of the choral text (with a subtle gap between the words *"To our"*) should have a similar articulation as the doubling strings.

201. In the Baroque, *basso seguente* means the traditional doubling of the lowest voice part by the organ. It is not always necessary to resort to this if the choir is sure of the notes. Moreover, when employed it is better to use the organ while the chorus basses are not singing, and save the harpsichord and double bass for the choral bass entry.

202. The musical language implies an obligatory trill for the sopranos (on the half cadence). But as this can be difficult for the choir, it is enough for the violins to trill while we ask the sopranos simply for a light accent, as mentioned in Appendix 4. This lets us highlight the close relationship between the accent (in keeping with the dynamic) and the trill (ornamentation). [Chapter 9 point 1]

203. The last two beats of bar 28 should be separated, for their 'harmonic rhythm': this relates more to the different chords implied than to the two different words.

204. A generous *messa di voce* on each of the long notes in the soprano line [Chapter 4, point 11].

If we place an arrow over the comma in bar 39 we do not lose energy.

205. An interesting example of differences in the writing, in no way alien to the Baroque practise of approximate notation (bar 55). We ask ourselves whether we should choose the rest in the vocal parts or the longer note in the strings. We could also ask: did Handel not put a rest in the vocal parts.... for a breath? But we insist that the lack of utter precision is a characteristic of Baroque writing, with illuminating examples in Bach's cantatas, where the choral phrasing and the articulation indicated for the strings are often different.

206. The first note of this extract is just as much the first note of the brief *coda* that brings down the curtain on this scene as it is the last note of the previous phrase.

Duet *"O lovely peace"*

207. We suggest no break in the sound from the *D* rising to *E*.

208. There are various possible moments for a 'coroncina'. They should be chosen with taste and refinement.

Solo and Chorus *"Rejolce, O Judah"*

209. Another case for difficult phrasing, without resorting to mere stereotype.

210. Should one accent the high notes or not? We believe that at this moment, and at this point of the oratorio, it would be good to opt for the accents, but without letting the tension sag until the cadence in bar 14.

211. Unlike the violin quaver, the soloist has an upbeat of a crotchet. Justify this extra length with a good 'accumulative' *crescendo*, as if the initial *D* generates it own harmonic, the *A*.

212. Avoid accents on the quavers without their own syllable.

213. A *piano* moment will break the monotony of *mf*.

214. An audacious seventh (*C natural*), the furthest of the accessible harmonics for a trumpet in *D*.

215. An example of a possible elegant embellishment for the soloist.

216. This passage *alla corda*, because finally we have stepwise motion that portrays a solid 'conquest'.

217. We suggest the following asymmetrical distribution of accents.

218. The only justification of the unusual figure in the tenor and continuo parts at the end of bar 55 seems to be to prevent a drop in tension.

219. A brilliant, very percussive passage, almost anticipating Poulenc or Bartok.

220. The strings should imitate the effect of the previous example.

221. Give the trumpet part rhythm (see example 197).

Here are two examples of how we may enrich the trumpet rhythm.

E. OBSERVATIONS UNDER THE MICROSCOPE

We shall analyse two numbers of *Judas Maccabeus* with greater detail than in the previous 221 examples, under a more powerful microscope: a Chorus and an Aria.

The ultimate objective would be to be able to justify every single note of the composition: to understand their function and deduce their interpretation. To take complete command of the work and…rewrite it! (metaphorically).

It is said that Mozart used to entertain himself by copying string quartets, but leaving out the original viola part to force himself to work out his own version of the part. This is the attitude that we would like to encourage, to break down the barrier between composer and director.

E.1 Chorus *"Lead on"*

7
Vl. I.
Vl. II.
Vla.
Ob. I.
Ob. II.
S.
Ju - dah disdains, Ju - dah dis- dains The gall- ing load of hos - tile chains,
A.
dains The gall - ing load of hos- tile chains, of hos - tile chains, Ju - dah disdains The gall - ing
T.
dains The gall- ing gall- ing, gall- ing load, the gall- ing load of hos - tile chains, Ju- dah disdains The gall - ing
B.
Ju- dah disdains the gall- ing, gall- ing load, the gall- ing load of hos - tile chains, Ju- dah disdains The gall - ing
B.C.
10
Vl. I.
Vl. II.
Vla.
Ob. I.
Ob. II.
S.
Lead on, lead on, Ju - dah disdains The gall - ing load of hos - tile
A.
load of hos - tile chains, Lead on, lead on, Ju-dah disdains The gall - ing load of hos- tile
T.
load of hos - tile chains, Lead on lead on, Ju- dah dis-dains The gall- ing load of hos- tile
B.
load of hos - tile chains, Lead on, lead on. Ju - dah dis - dains The gall - ing load of hos - tile
B.C.

13
Vl. I.
Vl. II.
Vla.
Ob. I.
Ob. II.
S.
chains, Lead on, lead on Ju - dah disdains The gall - ing load of hos - tile chains, the load of
A.
chains, Lead on, Ju - dah disdains The gall - ing load of hos - tile chains, the load of
T.
chains, Lead on, lead on, Ju- dah disdains The gall - ing load of
B.
chains, Lead on, lead on, Ju - dah dis dain The gall - ing load of
B.C.
16
Vl. I.
Vl. II.
Vla.
Ob. I.
Ob. II.
S.
hos - tile chains, Lead on, lead on, Ju - dah dis - dains The gall - ing load of
A.
hos - tile chains, Lead on, lead on, Ju - dah dis - dains The gall - ing load of
T.
hos - tile chains, Lead on, lead on, Ju - dah dis - dains The gall - ing load of
B.
hos - tile chains Lead on, lead on, Juh-dah dis- dains The gall - ing load of
B.C.

Bar 1: The massive chords serve to call the public to attention, with the appearance of the *turba* (chorus of the crowd, present in all oratorios and in the *Passions*). The chorus basses execute their *arpeggio* with brilliance in the style of tympani.

Bar 2: The oboes join with the agitation of someone arriving late, and with that accumulation of energy. The third beat develops into a half-cadence in the dominant, interrupting the triumphant *arpeggio* in D. Out of this moment of flexion emerges the bass statement, surprisingly *a capella*, perhaps so that the important content of the text is not obscured by the instruments.

Bar 3: The higher notes of the basses coincide with the key words (*disDAINS/ LOAD*), while the note on the most dramatic utterance (*HOStile*) is dotted, that is to say longer, to hold the attention.

Bar 4: The contralto and bass parts move in contrary motion, symbolizing the form of an embrace. The tenor part avoids the *D* on the syllable *"-dains"*. This *D* would have been the more logical melodic resolution, but it would have stolen the emphasis from the *D* on *"galling"*.

Bar 5: The interrupted cadence generates more impulse. And significantly it is at this very moment that the strings enter.

Bar 6: The use of imitation in *stretta* conveys anxiety, disturbance.

Bar 7: We have nothing to say. This is bad! If the conductor cannot find anything special to draw to our attention, or subtly to underline…and so, during our concert, this bar will pass by as an empty moment, neither condemned nor praised.

(In all honesty it has to be admitted that this is a rather conventional bar. We can only observe that, in order to break up the regularity, the soprano entry in bar 7 is delayed in relation to the rapid succession of the other vocal entries of the preceeding bar, as if Handel had wanted to bring out the entry of the upper part, which always gives the musical texture extra brilliance. But…would this be enough to make the whole bar interesting?)

Bar 8: Now the crux of the text (on the fourth beat) is on the second degree… and with an expressive suspension in the bass.

Bar 9: The semiquaver figure and the dotted rhythm in the altos and tenors serve as a mini-pause before regaining impulse.

Bar 10: The high notes in the violins prefigure the brilliant soprano entry.

Bar 11: At last, an emphatic homophonic rhythm in all parts.

Bar 12: The first and second beats are equal, with obsessive efficiency.

Bar 13: A bar with greater harmonic variety is needed. In our enthusiasm we can ignore the fifths between the bass and tenor lines (or perhaps Handel is saying that the people, in the heat of the crowd, forget their good contrapuntal manners…).

Bar 14: A device recalling the renaissance (in the two upper voices, as in a *bicinia* by Lassus).

Bar 15: The entire bar serves to accumulate energy up to the climax of the third beat of bar 16. This is increased by the leaps of a fourth and, in the second violins, of an octave!

Bar 16: The climax coincides with the high notes in the second violins and the 7-6 suspension. As a judicious moment of relief, this is followed by a brief general pause for the quaver rest.

Bar 17: Emphatic reiterations alternate dominant and tonic, like timpani.

Bar 18: Here, on the other hand, the subdominant and tonic alternate, as if regathering before the dissonant climax on the second beat of bar 19.

Bar 19: Effects already seen (bar 8). We are unable to explain the leap in the viola part (the high *D* could have been avoided with a calm *A* instead) other than that Handel may have wanted a strong accent at this point. If we are unable to explain this note, our lack of understanding will be noticed in the concert!… or we will have to come up with another idea for a future edition.

Bar 20: Put an arrow leading to the high *D* in the first violin (a leap that is otherwise difficult to explain), to emphasise an overwhelming excess.

Bar 21: Having used a fairly rudimentary harmony up till now (warlike chords), here every quaver needs a new chord: rounding off the scene and bringing down the curtain with this effective variant in the harmonic rhythm.

Bar 22: We feel that a short, accented note gives the idea of something confident and conclusive.

In summary, we have not been able to explain EVERY note… but our microscope has revealed more detail. There is still work to do!

Now, with similar criteria, we will try to explain every bar of a solo Aria.

E.2 Aria *"Ah! Wretched Israel"*

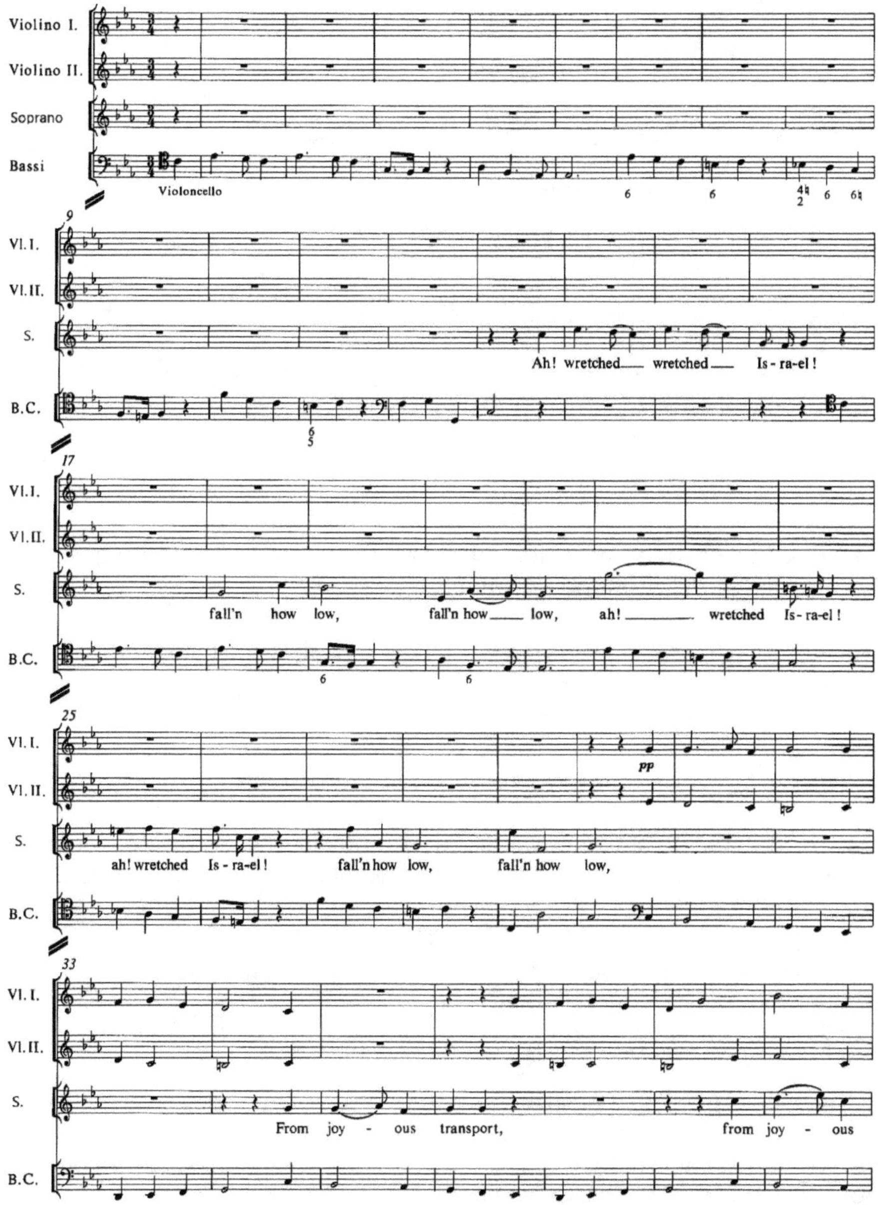

Sigue el coro.

The solo voice begins on the tonic, but not with the **relief** of the beginning of the bar, but in the **torment** of an upbeat.

The distribution of the text in bars 14 and 15, against the beat (inherited from Monteverdi), juxtaposes a pseudo-rhythm of 6/8 with the 3/4 of the continuo. This is a representation of **unease**.

Bar 16: The C minor arpeggio rests on the fifth: **instability**.

Bar 18: The soloist continues where she left off, with the same note, and a leap of **surprise** on "*how*" falling back not to B *natural* but to B *flat*: **anguish**.

Bar 20: The same mood, but with great **sadness** and **resignation** (thanks to the low *tessitura* and the suspending of the text on the hanging note).

Bar 22: The high note is a **cry**.

Bar 23: the chord falls: **collapse**.

Bar 24: "*Israel*", that word of greatest import, always has this dotted rhythm, like something incomplete: **precariousness**.

Bar 25: The first grade chord on the seventh delineates **drama**, and the oscillation *E-F-E-F* outlines **consternation**.

Bar 26: Here the fall of Israel is marked by a heavy feeling of **defeat**.

Bar 27: The form of bar 18 is inverted: **change**.

Bar 29: Here the leap of a seventh is that of final **disintegration**.

Bar 35: The new textual phrase adopts a syllabic setting in contrast to the opening: **hope**.

Bar 39: We modulate for a few moments to the major: **faith**.

Bar 40: The word "*transport*" has an almost meta-linguistic dimension, stretching the phrase: **courage**.

Bar 41: This is the bar with the most harmonic rhythm because each beat corresponds to a new chord: **overall vision**, for a very brief moment an optimistic outlook.

Bar 42: The soloist sings this single syllable, insistently onomatopoeic: **defeat**.

From here onwards, in the few bars that close this aria, the characteristics repeat, but rhythmically more anxious: **desperation**.

And, because a single cry is not enough, the chorus follows, with identical text and feeling.

F. APPENDICES

The following thematic sketches should be seen not merely from an acoustic point of view but also from a more 'philosophical' viewpoint.

Remember that in Baroque times musicians boasted a strong humanistic streak and considered themselves to be 'thinkers', and in the face of their work we should dare a less unilateral approach but one closer to the spirit of the age.

Bach, Handel, Telemann, in common with all their colleagues, occupied themselves in literature, mathematics and history. Today, specialized study (in whatever branch of knowledge) does not allow for this 'panoramic' cultural attitude.

And in the field of music we are also much more limited than in past times: suffice to say that a baroque musician could play several instruments, sang, composed and improvised!

F.1 Meta-linguistics

Baroque language uses various idioms, many present in extended works, and in those with dramatic character like oratorios.

We suggest various sources: the "Teoria degli Affetti", the fascinating discipline called *Musical Rhetoric* and illustrated texts like the pioneering work of A. Schweitzer (1955) or the enlightening book by Deryck Cooke (1959) *The Language of Music*.

As we have said in Chapter 3, BEFORE consulting these brilliant books we must ask ourselves:

What effect might the following figure represent?

And, reciprocally, how might one imagine that a baroque musician describes TEARS?

For the sake of curiosity, let us look at a couple of moments that invite a strongly allusive interpretation. As, for example, when Handel anticipates *ante litteram* forms which later on have been successfully adopted in the general musical literature. In the oratorio *Susanna* (1749) destiny threatens the protagonist with these notes (Recitative "*What means this weight that in my bosom lies?*")

What should we do? Maintain a certain naïf disengagement…or emphasise the its Beethovenian expressiveness?

Another example: Handel plays very audaciously with an advanced sonority. Again in *Susanna*, when the protagonist foresees her tragic fate…this chord appears in the strings (Aria *"If bloodless guilt be your intent"*):

with all the registers inverted!

F.2 Tuning

This area needs a different approach to that traditionally taken when dealing with romantic repertoire.

With an 18th century approach we learn of the following variables:

a. equal temperament (the octave subdivided into 12 identical semitones) and, paradoxically

b. the tendency to tune the 'difficult' notes higher (for instance we take the *G sharp* higher than the *A flat*).

In contrast, as is shown in the mine of information available in the treatises of the time, we can summarise very briefly that in the Baroque:

    a.   there exists an infinite number of tuning systems (*Werkmeister, Kirnberger,* ecc.).

    b.   the sharps are lower than their flat enharmonic neighbours.

This respects **relative tuning** (the intervals). Regarding **absolute tuning**, it is worth saying that the Baroque A in the 18th century was not at 440Hz but generally at 415Hz, or even lower, as in France (392Hz). Therefore, if we approach our investigation with the subtle distinctions of era and geography in mind, we will come across a wide variety of circumstances.

F.3 The role of Improvisation

Improvisation is the mother of inventive ornamentation. Without the practice of improvisation, ornamentation becomes mere imitation, an academic exercise.
So it is very important to practice this skill. One could begin to practice with *Grounds*, ostinato basses, *Chaconnes*.

In some cases the score seems to encapture a moment purely of improvisation, like a special effect in a modern film.
For instance, in Handel's oratorio *Susanna* we find the following bars (21 onwards) occurring at a very dramatic moment in the story. This schematic passage, written only for the continuo, has a descriptive rather than a musical function, and is in truth a sketch that seems to say: "add here a frenetic, percussive and obsessive improvisation".

In the end we must remember that a good interpretation of the solo roles needs the freshness of improvisation. And an attitude of airy improvisation will allow the conductor, in performance, to assume the identity of the composer, as if creating 'in real time'.
The less one has the feeling of an intermediary, the greater will be the emotion transmitted to those being conducted, and to those listening.

F.4 Ornaments, their implications and equivalents

Ornaments and dynamics often coincide, indistinguishably balancing or replacing each other.

a.   In many cases I can substitute an accent for a trill, and vice versa. Similarly, a 'finger vibrato' in a wind instrument (*flattement* in French music) is equivalent to a crescendo.
b.   A long note might need elegant and rather lavish ornamentation; if not, I could substitute a dazzling *crescendo*.

In either case I ask myself: which can I resort to with the greater ease and conviction, ornamentation or dynamic? And so, choose.

F.5 Examples of ornamentation

From Quantz's formidable treatise (1752: 223) there is a detailed example:

Quick movements can also lend themselves to ornamentation, especially in the form of variations called '*Double*'. There are many examples by Bach, Mattheson, Handel.... Here we include one of our own, for a movement from a Sonata by Telemann.

Original version:

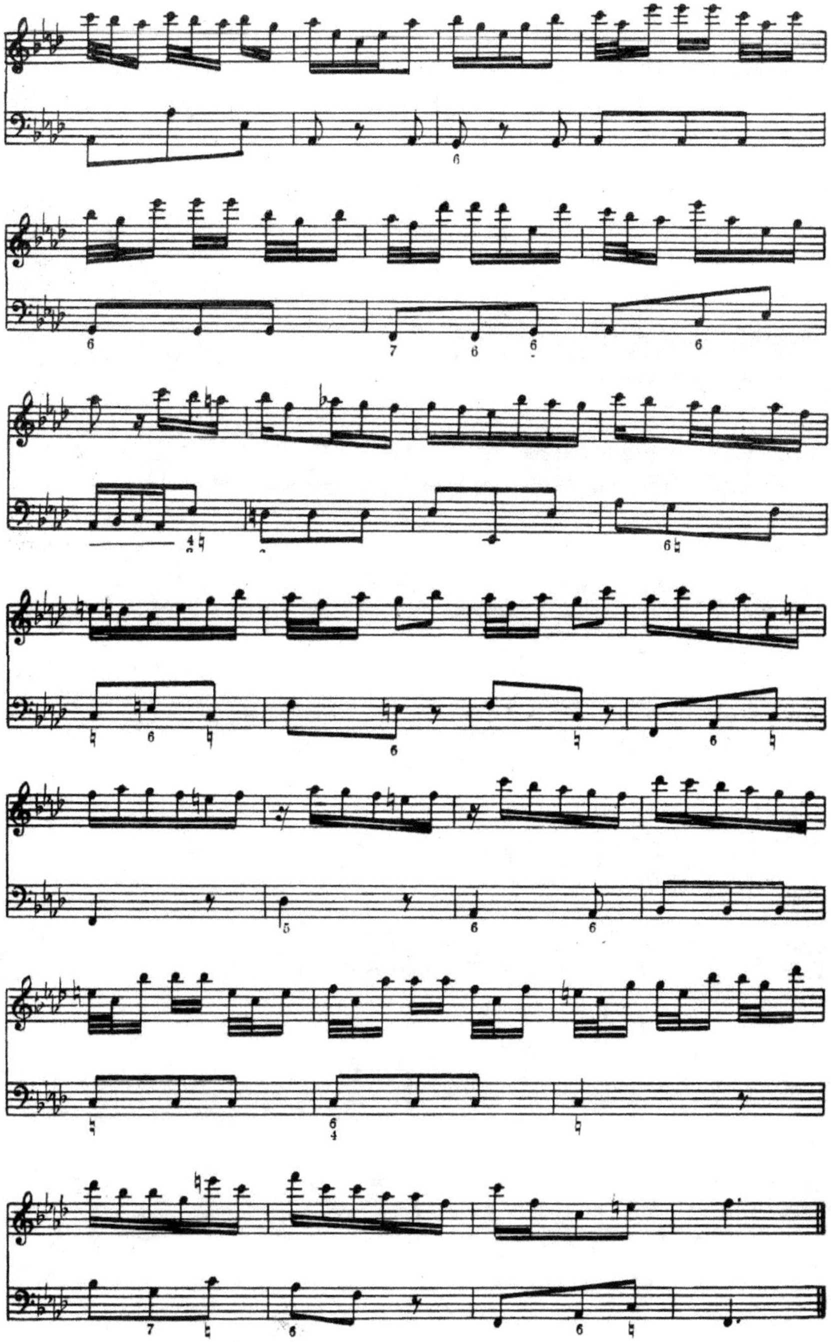

Double:

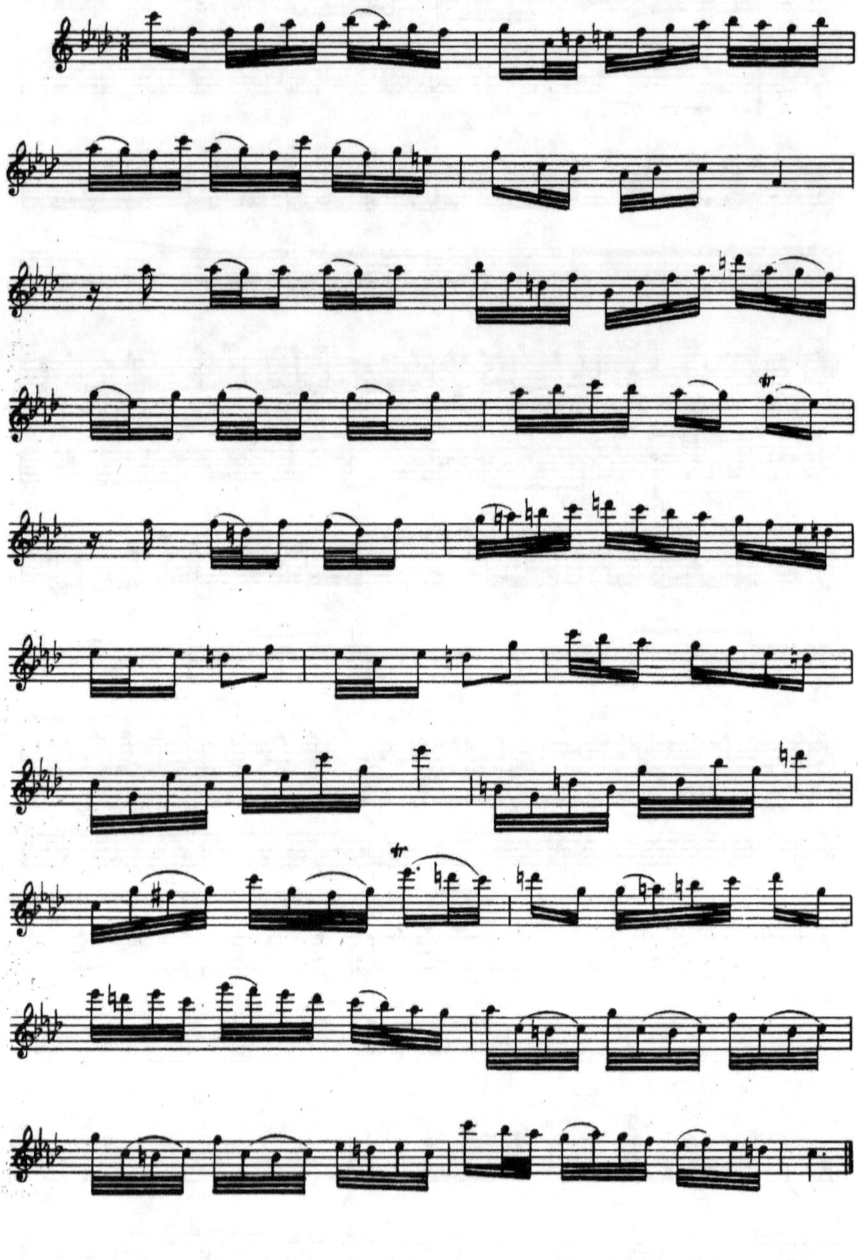

Aria from Telemann's Lukaspassion,1744

Embellishments by Philip Salmon, Tenor[1]

---

[1] Translator of this english version of the book

15
T
mine, e - ver lov - ing, let me be for e - ver
mein, ew' - ge Lie - be, laß mich nicht ver - lo - ren
Pno.
18
T
Thine. Thou in
sein. Du, O
Pno.
21
T
e - ver - last - ing mer - cy, e - ver lov - ving Sa - viour
e - wi - ges er - bar - men, ew' - ge Lie - be scho - ne
Pno.
24
T
mine, Sa - viour mine, Sa - viour mine, let me be for
mein, scho - ne mein, scho - ne mein, laß mich nicht ver -
Pno.
26
T
e - ver Thine. e - ver lov - ing, Sa - viour
lo - ren sein, ew' - ge Lie - be scho - ne
Pno.

29
T
mine, let me be for e - - - - - ver
mein, laß mich nicht ver - lo - - - - ren
Pno.
31
T
Thine.
sein.
Pno.
34
T
Pno.
37
T
Hear a sin - ner's poor con - fes - sion, look Thou
Willst du ja ein Ur - teil spre - chen, so sich'
Pno.
39
T
not on my trans - gres - sion, heal me by Thy
nicht auf mein ver - bre - chen, sich' auf mei - ne
Pno.

41

grace   di - vine,   look   not   on   my   trans - gres   -   sion,
Reu'   al - lein,   sich' nicht auf   mein   ver - bre   -   chen,

43

heal   me   by   Thy   grace_____   ,   by   Thy
sich'   auf   mei - ne   Reu'_____   ,   auf   mei - ne

46

grace   di   -   vine.
Reu   -   al   -   lein.

50

Thou   in
Du,   O

52

e   -   -   ver - last   -   sting   mer - cy,   e   -   ver
e   -   -   wi - ges   er - bar - men,   ew'   -   ge

54
T
lov - - ving Sa - - viour mine, let me be for
Lie - - be scho - ne mein, laß mich nicht ver -
Pno.
56
T
e - - - - - ver Thine, Sa - viour mine, Sa - viour mine, e - ver lov - ving,
lo - - - - - ren sein, scho - ne mein, scho - ne mein, ew' - ge Lie - be,
Pno.
59
T
let me be for e - - - - - ver Thine.
laß mich nicht ver - lo - - - - - ren sein.
Pno.
62
T
Thou in e - ver - last - ing
Du, O e - wi - ges er -
Pno.
65
T
mer - cy, e - ver lov - ving Sa - viour
bar - men, ew' - ge Lie - be scho - ne
Pno.

67
T
mine, Sa - viour mine, Sa - viour mine, let me be for
mein, scho - ne mein, scho - ne mein, laß mich nicht ver -
Pno.
69
T
e - - - - ver Thine, e - ver lov - ving Sa - viour
lo - - - - ren sein, e - ge Lie - be scho - ne
tr
Pno.
72
T
mine, let me be for e - - - - - - - - ver
mein, laß mich nicht ver - lo - - - - - - - ren
Pno.
74
T
Thine.
sein.
Pno.
77
T
Pno.

F.6 Bowing

Here we present some examples taken from the oratorio *Judas Maccabeus*, to address the exhausting challenge of thinking about and placing the bowing. Whoever enjoys Sudoku is sure to enjoy this job as well! There is a double satisfaction for those who are not string virtuosos: analyzing the work and dissecting it in detail, and so acquiring the necessary authority over string players... ever disposed to show up an unprepared conductor!

One should understand and think in the language of the string player, to avoid unnecessary discussions during rehearsals (chronically limited by that tyrant, time!). Very often a modification in the bowing helps the musicality of an uninteresting passage. What is more, good organization of the bowing improves the disposition of instrumentalists that I am conducting, showing that I know what I am doing and that I have prepared an objective for the rehearsal. As we have already said, an empty score is not much with respect to one that already has a few indications marked by my pencil.

We know that the needs of romantic music brought changes to the shape of the bow and the way it is employed. The older bows have a very pronounced outward curve (like a true bow), while modern and present-day bows are slightly curved inwards. Their length and weight are also very different as baroque bows are much shorter and lighter! The weight and length of a baroque bow can be 'emulated' by a modern bow by placing it on the string 10 cm further away from the heel.

In this way the famous 18th century *legato*, in which a single bow-stroke sustains the sound of many notes (our paradigmatic *melisma*), is replaced as a general stylistic practice by a simple (but expressive) *detaché*: every note is played with a different bow-stroke. This allows us to control the intensity, articulation and movement of each sound, so that our *melisma* is free and varied, in contrast to the homogenous and conventional 18th century *legato*.

Let us explore a few examples of our own suggestions of baroque bowing, in relation to the modern bowing called for by traditional Romanticism, to learn from the comparison.

Some basic criteria:

- The bow is 'pulled': used when starting on the beat. This way of moving the bow, in the same direction as gravitational pull, implies a certain accentuation or explosion of sound appropriate for loud moments. It is also called the "down bow", and is shown by this symbol:

- The bow is 'pushed': especially used for the upbeat, as this way of passing the bow goes against gravity and so makes the attack light with a subtle *crescendo*. We can also establish for this movement an analogy with arsis (strong beat - inhalation, renewed energy), and for its opposite thesis (weak beat - exhalation, relaxation of energy).
  Generally this is called the 'up bow', the opposite of the movement we have just described. It is shown by this sign:

  V

- In polyphony, give the same bowing scheme to each instrument that plays the theme, even when one instrument holds a note longer than the other instruments.
- In homophony, arrange the bowing to obtain a homogenous pattern, even when one instrument has several notes more than the others.
- We should note on every player's part only the changes in bowing that modify the normal up and down of the bow. If there is an upbeat of just one note, the player will know that his first stroke will be an up bow, and so we do not need to mark it in. Instead we should mark all the bowing in our own score, so that we can easily locate the position of all the bows when repeating any fragment in rehearsal.
- A slur '*di arco*' (embracing a sequence of various notes in a single bow) is considered an embellishment, an exception (as we have already said of vibrato). Use it with care.
- In the end, it would be better to be able rely on 'clean' orchestral parts, free of any editorial direction and so ready for our pencil. Normally the orchestral material has modifications or additions in relation to the original, brought by editorial revisions or…by other musicians who have already used the parts. So the first job to do is to remove from the parts any sign extraneous to the strictly musical score.

1.   An example taken from the overture to Judas Maccabeus helps us to visualise how to execute passages of this nature, common in overtures in the French style. We can give it a bold and solemn character by separating every long note from the following short note, and joining this to the following long note. The first note of the bar does not need an indication because by convention it is a down bow.

Baroque articulation

Modern articulation

2. Still in the Overture, in this passage, 'retaking' the bow (which means two down bows across the bass) will create a *caesura* between the first and second notes; moreover with a valid accent on it. This is an interesting moment in this polyphonic extract, where the violins join the violas in a rhythmic unity that accents the second beat of the bar!

3. The semiquavers constitute the smallest note values in the Overture. Therefore, as we said in Chapter 5, point 3, this will be the value to play with a *portato*; a conflicting articulation with respect to 'modern' performance, in which the smallest note values are usually played *staccato*.

In bar 119 the *melisma* is replaced by repeated notes: here the function becomes rhythmical, and so its articulation is more separated, like a *staccato*

4. In the Chorus preceeding the Aria *"Arm, arm ye brave"* we find the rhythm of a gallop mentioned in example 82. To reinforce the percussive effect of the semiquavers, we suggest retaking the down bow at the beginning of every group. In modern performance, a similar passage would probably be played with a *jetté*, lightening off. According to the criteria in Chapter 5, point 3, the crotchets are *staccato*. The same applies to the crotchets, unless the melodic shape moves in stepwise fashion.

5. In the Chorus *"Lead on, lead on"* we see one of the most frequent uses of the strings: doubling the voices. As the sung text does not appear in the instrumental parts (although it would be a nice addition to offer this information by writing it in), we should unify the articulation and the dynamics with the pronunciation and prosody of the text.

Therefore the first violin part needs the following notation:

with which we try to arrange the bowing so that accented syllables are played with a down bow. To do this we can leave the accents that come from the normal flow of the bow as in bar 7, because here they coincide with the text (the **V** symbol on the *D* is added to avoid slurring to the crotchet as might be normal in cases like this). A different case presents itself in bar 8, where we give the same movement to the bow for the two quavers, to arrive at the accent on the third, as required by the text (*"galling"*). A similar situation appears in bar 9.

6. Let us now look at an example from the Chorus *"Disdainful of danger"*:

At bar **34** we have a passage like that described in example 103: a figure that requires a particular bow stroke. The bowing in the triple-time bars generally needs particular attention because, being uneven in rhythm, they will tend to run on with bowing 'as it comes'. We recommend alternating an up bow in one bar with a down bow in the next.

Therefore we suggest the following bowing:

As can be seen, for the same rhythmic shape we use the same bowing scheme. We shall change at bar 35, because there are three quavers, and at bar 40, where it is necessary to accent the second beat, being on a chord of the dominant (and we can also embellish it with a tastefully applied trill).

Unnecessary markings can be avoided as the player will understand that when the shape is the same, so is the bowing pattern. So we need to mark the bowing only in bars 34, 35 and 40.

7. In the Chorus *"Fallen is the foe"* we have this *incipit*:

To start the first violin semiquavers comfortably we must indicate that the quavers should be bowed upwards, ie. 'pushed'. For the rest of the instruments we adopt the same criteria, because even though they don't continue to play in the first bar, in the second bar they have a similar pattern. And so we mark the first violin part like this:

As a precaution we have added brackets around the low *D* because it falls on the strong beat with a down bow and so will be prone to an accent, almost by default (see example 189).

In any case, we have the option of not changing the direction of the bow on the quavers but on the second semiquaver instead, which, like the first one, will be an up bow.

As we have seen, this example illustrates very well the possible variations in the distribution of the bowing.

8.   In the same Chorus, we find the fugue "*Where war-like Judas wields his righteous sword*":

In passages such as this one, where the dynamics are completely determined by the text, we would articulate with the bow 'as it comes', but marking every note with hairpins, commas, symbols of non-accentuation etc. (see Lessons 4 and 5). As the speed is rather moderate it would be too much to retake the bow on every word or syllable (see example 4 in this section).

9.   The beginning of the Aria "*How vain is man who boasts in fight*" is in an off-beat rhythm, where the slurs might not be considered an effective bowing pattern. They would be valid only if accompanied by a *diminuendo* (remembering our example of the word Ba-roc-co, Chapter 5, point 4). Or, for clarity, we could leave out the slurs and mark the bowing in such a way as to obtain the same dynamics:

Another option could be to slur the trills in bars 3 and 4 (ie. the last three notes of the bar).

10. In the second part of the same Aria we find a bow stroke that is prototypical of the baroque era (which we will next encounter only in works composed in the 20th century!), the *vibrato d'arco*:

This effect/mood stands in the case of long notes with their subdivision into smaller note values. To produce this effect, the player should place the bow on the string as it is written, but without completely lifting it between one note and the next. The effect obtained is that of a long note accented according to the subdivisions (see also its use in the Sonata of the Cantata *"Ad genua"* of *Membra Jesu Nostri* by Buxtehude – 1680, or in works by Kuhnau).

In modern performance this notation would have a simply visual effect, where the four slurred notes would be played by the bow moving in the same direction, but separated by lifting it.

11. In the Aria "Ah! Wretched Israel", we find this passage:

At bar 31 we have a rhythmic shape already mentioned in examples 6 and 9 of this section, in this case translated into crotchets and quavers. We take the same decisions regarding the bowing.

At bar 33, as we have already shown (bearing in mind the comments at example 116), the rhythm suggests a minuet. Therefore we use a special bowing pattern, applying one of the few slurs that we feel to be necessary. As with any baroque slurring, it implies a *diminuendo* followed by a *caesura*.

12. In the Chorus that accompanies the Aria in the previous example, we see a similar situation:

We suggest bowing derived from the chorus:

13. Now let us look at the following passage from the Aria "*The Lord worketh wonders*":

To preserve a regular bowing towards the low note on the strong beats, we place a down bow on the first semiquaver in bar 7. We also put a cautionary sign on the quaver that begins the scale, to avoid the brusque 'hiccup' effect of lifting the bow from the string. As we have just noted in example 3, the semiquavers, being of the smallest value, will be *portate*. As a consequence, the quavers will be *staccato*. We can establish a little convention: the quaver that preceeds a group of semiquavers is 'infected' with the same articulation and therefore becomes longer. We call this form, 'retrospective articulation'.

At bar 8 the bow moves 'as it comes' until the cadence, where the bowing is adjusted so as to head towards the low note.

14. Another case of minuet rhythm appears in the Aria *"Wise men, flattering, may deceive us"*:

In the first bar we have changed the bow on the first semiquaver, so that the trill is on an up bow in order to arrive on the first beat of the second bar with a down bow.

15. At the beginning of the duet "O lovely peace" we find a pastoral dance:

Given its placid character, inferred from the text, this is a good moment to think about *legato* (several notes played with one bow stroke). With just one adjustment (in bar 1) the bowing gains fluidity and consistency, and so no more markings are needed. So, the first note of bar 1 will be the conventional down bow (on the strong beat), and to arrange the rest of this passage we keep the bow moving in the same direction for the following quaver. This way we achieve the correct alternation of the remaining bow strokes.

Thanks to these brief examples we can see that, while in Romanticism it is the player's left hand (the one that touches the strings) that is expressive (vibrato, glissando, harmonics etc.), in the Baroque the expressive inflections are centred on the right hand.

BIBLIOGRAPHY:

BUKOFZER, Manfred, *La música de la época barroca. De Monteverdi a Bach* [1947], Madrid, Alianza editorial, 1986.

COOKE, Derek, *The language of music*, Oxford, Oxford University Press, 1959.

DAHLHAUS, Carl, *Fundamentos de historia de la música* [1977], Barcelona, Gedisa, 1997.

DONINGTON, Robert, *Baroque Music: Style and Performance*, London, Faber Music, 1982.

DOLMETSCH, Arnold, *The Interpretation of the Music of the Seventeenth and Eighteenth Centuries revealed by Contemporary Evidence*, London and Seattle, University of Washington Press/Novello, 1915.

RIEMANN, Hugo, *System der musikalischen Rhthmik und Metrik* [1903], Parte 2, Vaduz, Sändig Reprint Verlag, 1993.

RINK, John, *La interpretación musical* [2002], Madrid, Alianza editorial, 2006.

ROTSCHILD, Fritz, *The Lost Tradition in Music*, London, Adam & Black, 1953.

ROTTMANN, Kurt, *"La interpretación de la música barroca"*, en Revista Musical Chilena, vol. 14, n° 72, Santiago de Chile, 1960.

SOURCES:

BACH, C. P. E., *Versucht über die wahre Art das Clavier zu spielen*, Berlin, Henning, 1753.

BEMETZRIEDER, Anton, *Leçons de clavecin, et principes d'harmonie*, Paris, Bluet, 1711.

BROSSARD, Sebastien de, *Dictionnaire de musique*, Paris, Ballard, 1703.

CACCINI, Giulio, *Le nuove musiche*, Firenze, Marescotti, 1602.

COUPERIN, François, *L'Art de toucher le clavecin*, Paris, Ed. del autor, 1716.

FANTINI DA SPOLETI, G., *Modo per imparare a sonare di tromba*, Frankfurt, D. Vuastch, 1638.

MATTHESON, Johann, *Der vollkommene Capellmeister (el completo Maestro de capilla)*, 1739: http://imslp.org/wiki/Der_vollkommene_Capellmeister_ (Mattheson,_Johann)

MOZART, Leopold *Método de tocar el violín* [1765], Copia manuscrita en castellano, en Música, Revista del Conservatorio Real de Madrid n° 12-13, 2006.

QUANTZ, Joachim, *Trattato sul flauto traverso* [1752] (Sergio Balestracci ed.), Libreria Musicale Italiana Editrice, 1992.

The Authors

Sergio Siminovich
Having gained his Diploma in Orchestral Conducting and his PhD in Arts in the Faculty of Fine Arts at the *Universidad Nacional de La Plata* (Argentina), he completed his studies in France with Jean-Pierre Rampal; at the University of Nottingham, and at the Guildhall School of Music, London (United Kingdom); and at the Royal Conservatoire in The Hague (Netherlands). He specialized in baroque oratorio with Francis Baines, Philip Picket and John Alldis.
In 1991 he founded the *Sociedad Handel* in Buenos Aires where he is Artistic Director.
In 1996 he was appointed Director of the *Coro Polifonico Provinciale de Santa Fe*, a post he still holds.
He holds the Chair as Professor in Ordinary of Choral Direction in the Faculty of Fine Arts at the Universitad Nacional de La Plata. From 1989 to 1990 he held the title of Chair of Philiological Interpretation of Baroque Music and of Continuo Realisation at the Conservatorio di Santa Cecilia in Rome. In Italy he has also taken the role of Director of the Coro da Camera of RAI. He has led numerous seminars on the interpretation of ancient music in Argentina, the United States, Switzerland, Italy, Spain and Brazil.

e-mail: sersiminovich@yahoo.com.ar

Rodrigo de Caso
Violinist, pianist and composer, he completed his studies on the Graduate Music Course in Composition in the Faculty of Fine Arts at the *Universidad Nacional de La Plata* (Argentina). He completed his composition studies at Georgia University (USA) with Leonard Ball.
Currently he holds the post of Assistant to the Chairman of Choral Direction III and Vocal and Instrumental Ensembles in Contemporary Musical Language in the Faculty of Fine Arts at the *Universidad Nacional de La Plata*.
As an instrumentalist and composer he is a member of the contemporary music ensemble *DAMus-IUNA* and of the *Sociedad Handel*, Buenos Aires. He collaborates closely with Sergio Siminovich in a variety of musical and educational projects.

e-mail: decaso.rodrigo@gmail.com

www.ingramcontent.com/pod-product-compliance
Lightning Source LLC
LaVergne TN
LVHW021713080426
835510LV00010B/983